THE
DIVERSITY
CULTURE

THE
DIVERSITY
CULTURE

Creating Conversations of Faith with Buddhist
Baristas, Agnostic Students, Aging Hippies,
Political Activists, and Everyone in Between

MATTHEW RALEY

Kregel
Publications

The Diversity Culture: Creating Conversations of Faith with Buddhist Baristas, Agnostic Students, Aging Hippies, Political Activists, and Everyone in Between

© 2009 by Matthew Raley

Published by Kregel Publications, a division of Kregel, Inc., P.O. Box 2607, Grand Rapids, MI 49501.

Scripture taken from the NEW AMERICAN STANDARD BIBLE, updated edition. Copyright © 1960, 1962, 1963, 1968, 1971, 1972, 1973, 1975, 1977, 1995 by The Lockman Foundation. Used by permission. (www.Lockman.org)

Library of Congress Cataloging-in-Publication Data
Raley, Matthew.
    The diversity culture : creating conversations of faith with Buddhist baristas, bohemian artists, agnostic students, aging hipsters, political activists, and everyone in between / Matthew Raley.
        p. cm.
    Includes bibliographical references.
    1. Missions. 2. Evangelistic work. 3. Discrimination—Religious aspects—Christianity. I. Title.
    BV2063.R35   2009   261.0973—dc22   2009001442

ISBN 978-0-8254-3579-9

Printed in the United States of America
09 10 11 12 13 / 5 4 3 2 1

For my parents, Steve and Cyndi Raley,
with love and gratitude.

CONTENTS

THE CHAIR IN CAFÉ SIDDHARTHA

A woman rolled over and reached, but remembered that her new friend had already left. She sat up, staring at the impression he had made on her bed. At least he had his own life.

Past cold candles she shuffled to her bathroom, the air inside still fragrant, condensation still clinging to the window after his shower. He would be wearing that Huntsman suit made for him last time he was in London—the suit he wore when she first saw him two weeks ago at Davies Symphony Hall. And maybe the same tie from Arnys. When you're on a team preparing to argue before the Ninth Circuit you don't wear your beloved tie-dye and jeans—even on Columbus Day.

The woman was annoyed that her new client had insisted on meeting. Even though the holiday is totally imperialist, she wished that she didn't have to get into business mode, and she was bored by the prospect of yet another menu-design. Still, the meeting wasn't until early afternoon, so she lingered over her makeup.

The TV remote called from the kitchen counter to her pre-election obsessions. She switched on MSNBC and caught the headlines. Weekend poll shows Obama up seven.[1] *Cool.* Europeans try to keep their banks from collapsing. *Not cool.*

She poured coffee out of the French press and held the mug under her nose while she scanned the *San Francisco Chronicle*. Predictions that the financial collapse will stall climate change initiatives, anxious summary of the economic developments over the weekend, analysis of McCain and Obama avoiding the immigration issue.[2]

After the computer finished clicking and sighing, she checked how much e-mail had piled up over the weekend. Amid the flurry of personal messages were two articles from the *New York Times*. One friend had bragging rights, a mention of the bookstore where he worked, City Lights, in a travel article on Buddhist attractions in San Francisco.[3] Another friend was gloating over Sarah Palin's splitting right-wingers, forwarding a column by David Brooks that dissed the Alaskan governor.[4] The friend wrote, "McSame's going down! You betcha!"

Time kept on slipping, slipping, slipping.

The woman opened a cupboard. *Froot Loops!* It was very cute. Her new friend had gone out this morning and brought back Froot Loops and put Toucan Sam just inside the cupboard smiling down his beak at her. She loved a guy who could keep an inside joke going. All weekend bumming around Half Moon Bay it had been, "Follow my nose! It always knows!"

But if he went any further with it, she'd get annoyed.

Attired in the black trousers and narrow-shouldered jacket she found in Milan, her funky boots that clopped on her wide floorboards, and a low-cut, fitted T-shirt, she strode out of her loft into the fog, down to her Outback.

At this hour, the drive along I-80 and across the Bay Bridge into the City would not be enraging but still long. That was why they had KQED. "Talk of the Nation" was all about lynching—"How Far Have We Come?" Ted Koppel was talking about his new documentary on the subject, and a congressman described his experiences as an eighteen-year-old Freedom Rider in Mississippi.[5] *Mississippi, where they still believe the Bible's commands to hate and kill people.* The woman glanced at a billboard against the proposition banning gay marriage. *We haven't come all that far, have we? Still fighting hate.*

She parked, slung her large leather portfolio over her shoulder, and walked to Café Siddhartha around the corner from her studio—as if she needed more caffeine. What she wanted was the aura of the place, the energy. It was like stepping into one of the temples where she'd meditated in Tibet. The walls were floor-to-ceiling saffron. Deep chimes spoke, and the Buddha laughed. The café had an authenticity she needed—in spite of the hissing espresso machine.

The woman took her mocha and turned to the seating area thronged with people. There was only one chair at a common table—right next to ... whoever this was.

Well, she knew exactly who he was: he was her mental picture of a Mississippi bigot. He was fat, his face all soft and oily. He wore this dark blue cardboard suit with the jacket buttoned over his paunch. And where could he have gotten it? And when? It could only have been Penney's, circa 1995, what with the wide lapels and sloping shoulders. This he had mated with a white shirt and skinny red tie—1984, Nancy Reagan red. And the pre-folded, matching pocket square.

His hair was Grecian Formula black, parted on the right by a razor blade and swirled above his forehead, apparently under thermonuclear heat.

He was reading a book by—no, surely not. It couldn't have been Nixon's Chuck Colson. But it was: his picture was on the back.

How was she to bask in the Tibetan aura sitting next to a Baptist? He reminded her of the imported southerner her parents' church hired in 1979 when she was in high school—Mississippi in the San Joaquin valley. Had he gotten lost passing out tracts at Pier 39? Really lost?

The Barriers

Many evangelicals fear this woman.

They don't know what to do with her hostility: confront, mock, soothe? There's no soothing an attitude so visceral. Confronting it is asking for hostility times ten. That leaves mockery—the talk radio mode most evangelicals have learned by now—which fire-bombs whatever bridge there might've been.

But the fear goes deeper. Many evangelicals sense the woman's hostility is the least of their problems.

Evangelicals in America have a distinct subculture. They tend to worship in churches with conservative political and theological views. The strongest bases of evangelicalism are in suburbia, and the movement is disproportionately white and middle class. Evangelicals have their own media, reading different books and magazines than secular people, visiting different Web sites, listening to Christian music and radio, and often watching Christian TV stations and movies.[6]

The woman, many evangelicals feel, has built a life in which they have no place. She didn't just stop going to church after escaping her parents; she moved to the big city and changed identities. Her adopted ways were a point-by-point rebuke to her inheritance—not small-town or suburban, but urban; not Western but Eastern; not Christian but New Age; not monogamous but liberated.

I believe the woman now lives in her own distinct culture, one that is full of paradox.

While her culture is often urban, it thrives just as powerfully in Boulder as in San Francisco. The culture is often highly educated and artistic, embracing the preacher's daughter who came out as a lesbian, went to Reed College in Portland, and became a visual artist. But it also belongs to the straight, blue-collar guy who, despite never finishing college, does well painting houses in Fresno, the guy whose history is unclear—the salt of the earth, but with a ponytail. While this culture is hostile to America's vast consumer society, rejecting mass-production aesthetics and corporate values, its adherents have well-tended investment portfolios and are influential in the business world, nurturing such successes as Ben & Jerry's and Starbucks. Yet Starbucks both appeals to and repels them (which is why our woman supports the independent café rather than hanging out at the chain). Politically the culture is blue: antiwar, environmentalist, pro–gay marriage, secular. But it consistently seeks to preserve local traditions.

This culture cries for a label. It needs to be distinguished from the consumer society, but a tag remains elusive. David Brooks calls it *Bobo*, "bourgeois bohemian." Bill O'Reilly calls it "secular progressive." Rush Limbaugh calls it "liberal wacko."

I call it the diversity culture, after its top priority. Café Siddhartha is about a convergence of influences, insights into life that come from exploration, openness, and freedom. The worst evil to the diversity culture is

> **The Diversity Culture**: The dominant American ethos of openness toward all beliefs and spiritual traditions.

bigotry. Every shelter for narrow thinking must be eroded by fresh winds.

Most evangelicals have difficulty penetrating this culture's ways, and seem to feel it was designed to exclude them. They feel the sting every time the woman talks about bigotry, not knowing whether to embrace the label or fight it. Multicultural talk is not merely irritating to them, but is insulting: "Diversity means every culture but ours." So the rise of the diversity culture, especially when it wins elections as it did in 2008 with the triumph of Barack Obama, fills them with fear—the fear of having to interact with someone who looks down on them.

Evangelicals as a group feel they don't belong in Café Siddhartha.

The barriers between the diversity culture and evangelicals are real. The hostility is not a misunderstanding, and the roots of it are often deep in the soil of family. The issues that have fed the hostility are consequen-

> **Siddhartha**: The Sanskrit birth name of the Buddha, translated, "One who has found meaning."

tial: disagreements about spirituality, cultural principles, history, politics, and the nature of free society. Mere dialogue will not make the hostility wither.

But evangelical fear can be dispelled—and must be.

Fear sabotages interactions with the woman of Café Siddhartha through pride, contempt, suspicion, and cynicism. Evangelicals' inferior status in the diversity culture's pecking order is often just as significant as the eclipse of their principles in provoking these emotions. They often react to Subaru

Outbacks and the *New York Times*. Fear and its comrades can make evangelicals petty.

In addition, the fear often drives evangelicals to a blanket rejection of every aspect of the diversity culture without asking enough questions. For example, the diversity culture is overwhelmingly on the political left, while evangelicals are mostly on the right. But progressive political views are not necessarily anti-Christian. Is evangelism about winning souls, or votes? Further, the diversity culture often looks down on middle class life, provoking defensiveness in evangelical suburbia. But middle class life is not inherently godly. Should evangelicals be willing to question their social assumptions? More deeply, evangelicals can easily brand an openness to new perspectives as "relativism." But is it relativistic to hear someone out, or to participate in discussions that may not resolve neatly?

The evangelical sense of calling in America needs to be refocused, which cannot be done wisely by reacting against the diversity culture in fear. The evangelical mission should be defined by God's call in Scripture.

Fear of the diversity culture is not just a barrier to interacting with those outside evangelicalism, but even with some inside. The fear can be a generational marker: young believers, coming of age under the dominance of diversity, often do not identify with older believers' suspicions. Truth be told, many young believers view the Baptist at Café Siddhartha from the same cultural point of view as the woman—fairly or unfairly. But they also sense that their heritage is a vital part of their calling to influence their secularized peers, and they desire wisdom from their elders about how to display Jesus Christ to a culture that will not acknowledge the category of Truth. Can older Christians impart that wisdom if they are fearful of interacting with Café Siddhartha?

There is an even more fundamental problem with evangelical fear. Amid similar conflicts, there was no such fear in Jesus.

The Model

A woman left her new friend's house with a water pot. She strolled south through her town of Sychar, built at the foot of the mountains and enclosed by a wall. In the open countryside, the woman passed the tomb of her fore-father, Joseph, whose bones were buried here when Joshua led God's people into the land. Shielding her eyes against the high sun, she gazed at the peak of Mt. Gerizim where she knew the same Joshua had built a sanctuary to Yahweh.[7]

The location was commanded by Moses, and her fathers had built a sec-ond temple there,[8] the very law carved on the stones of the altar.[9]

There was no sanctuary now. Almost two centuries before, John Hyrca-nus the Jew had leveled it, just as he had destroyed the capital Samaria and opened the countryside to be trampled by Galilean Jews on their way to the apostate temple in Jerusalem.[10] She dropped her arm and looked back at the road. Maybe she was divorced. Maybe she had precious little share in the hope of her fathers. But at least she wasn't a Jew.

Down the road she heard voices, Galilean voices. Loud men kicked up dust on their way north.[11] She was amid fields now, with no orchard in which to find shelter while they passed. And it was too late anyway. One of them had seen her, and the gang went silent. They spread across the width of the road as they walked; she would either have to push through them or step into the field. She chose the field, which at least gave her an excuse to look at her feet.[12]

In the shelter of Gerizim, amid trees, she approached the well of Jacob, the patriarch's legacy to Sychar. And who was this?

Another Jew—another Galilean, no doubt. Sitting at her father's well as if he owned it, as if Hyrcanus had given him the right to drink from it. Sitting there with his fringes, a rabbi, a professor of hate. Sitting there as if his presence would keep her from drawing water at her own well, as if she'd turn around and trudge back to Sychar with an empty jar. Well, he would be the one to leave.

The woman moved in close to the rabbi, looking at the well, tying the rope to her jar, lowering it and pulling it up—as if he wasn't there.

She felt his eyes on her. She heard the linen of his robe whisper as his hand reached into her peripheral vision. "Give me a drink."

A Galilean, all right. The accent gave him away. What fresh insult was this?

The Challenge

We have an easy response to Jesus' interactions at the well (John 4:1–26). He was God. He knew the Samaritan woman supernaturally, so he could take social risks with assurance. We're not divine. The best we can do is learn his compassion for the lost and be ready for any opportunities.

The easy response won't work.

The apostle John showed more of Jesus' interactions than any other witness. John gave us Jesus talking with Nicodemus in the dark (3:1–15), Jesus being confronted by his grieving friends Martha and Mary (11:17–44), Jesus in dialogue with his anxious disciples before his arrest (John 13–16), and Jesus being interrogated by Pilate (18:28–19:22).

John did not show these scenes to impress us with Jesus' divinity, but to refine our emulation of his humanity. Jesus the Galilean Jew initiated a relationship with the Samaritan woman. The offer of living water came from the Word made flesh. This conversation displays human hostility being conquered by human love.

So the tension at the well of Samaria can teach us to overcome fear at our own wells, the intersections where we meet the diversity culture.

The Premise

This book is about healing broken relationships as a way of showing Jesus Christ to contemporary America. My desire is that you find sound scholarship and thinking here. But, because of the book's relational focus, I realize that my observations are often subjective—a characteristic I do not regret, because the issues in this book are full of personal significance for me.

As a pastor, I feel the hostility between evangelicals and the diversity culture. Like every pastor traversing society's intersections, I constantly analyze how to minister to people across the boundaries of politics and status. I have to. If I do not find ways to cross the boundaries, I worry that in twenty years my church won't exist.

But I also feel the hostility more intuitively. As I will describe in the conclusion, I inherited from my parents a combination of strong views and openness to interaction. In a sense, my parents' habits and example have placed me at the well from the beginning of my life. I love the people of Café Siddhartha and the people of evangelical churches because I grew up around both. So the heat of their charges and countercharges is grievous to me. There are days when I don't care which side is right.

The spiritual conclusions of this book come from my own struggle to show Christ as I know him—strong and gracious—in the context of this hostility.

At eighteen, I went off to a secular university, taking my strong conservative views of politics and theology—views which I retain. Despite my relatively open upbringing, I had a sense of going to battle, of the need for unflinching confrontation with those who held other views. I was determined to live out my heritage in the midst of opposition.

But my stories about academic liberals, about the New Age movement, about the persecution of Christians on campuses weren't solid enough. I quickly found that I wasn't dealing with types, but with individuals. One day, after a session of the freshman course on worldviews, I was sent to the university chaplain for counseling. I had been "courageous for the truth" in class and thought sure I was in for some brainwashing. Instead the chaplain and I traded favorite scenes from Monty Python. When I took a course on the New Testament from a liberal religious studies professor, I expected nothing but ideology. But in class he gave a clearer and more disciplined exposition of the gospel from John 3 than I had ever heard from any evangelical preacher, and he responded to my criticisms of modernist interpretations with respect.

I needed to interpret people justly.

I had, for instance, a self-indulgent reactiveness to people's identity signals. The tie-dye, the clogs, the NARAL buttons, the academic lingo—all of it fed my sarcasm, the memory of which now embarrasses me. I also had a self-indulgent tendency to fill in what people believed on the basis of one or two statements, only to find that their views were more subtle than I had imagined. My self-indulgence even allowed me a superior attitude toward people's experiences. A friend once shared his view that rape was an expression of male dominance, a view I dismissed as feminist cant. When, in a cold fury, he told me how men back in his rural hometown bragged about their exploits, I shut up. He had been exposed to talk more vile than I'd ever heard.

For God to use me in the diversity culture, I had to confront my self-indulgence, and learn how to be godly in the midst of opposition.

So this book is the fruit of my study and struggle, and might be understood best as a kind of testimony, even confession, rather than an argument. For the past several years I have tried to learn how Jesus is converting the diversity culture, and like others wrestling with these issues, I have not found many models. There were moments in this intellectual and relational struggle when I've never felt more alone.

I am qualified only to document what I've observed at the intersections between evangelicals and the diversity culture, and to draw applications that I have found to be powerful from the model of Jesus Christ.

My method is twofold: First, I try to let the diversity culture speak for itself, even to choose the topics of discussion. I do this using selections from the "Most E-mailed" list of articles on the *New York Times* Web site in 2006–2008. The list, especially from that news organization, is one way to answer the question, "What issues does the diversity culture think about?" Second, I intend to construct a detailed analogy between the Samaritan-Jewish hostility and the Siddhartha-evangelical hostility. I believe that if we consider Jesus' interactions with the Samaritan woman carefully, we can understand how he is interacting today.

In part 1, I give a tour of four barriers that I've noticed between the diversity culture and evangelicals. But an exegesis of culture is not enough for evangelicals to cross those barriers. So, in part 2, I outline a theology for healing relationships today, what I believe is the gospel of John's winning message. In part 3, I offer four practical guides from Jesus' interaction with the Samaritan woman.

I believe we have the opportunity to heal relationships with people of the diversity culture, and I base that belief on a simple premise: We have made a mistake by interpreting both the woman and the Baptist according to their group identities. *Today, the individual is more credible than the group.*

BECOMING A HEALER

- Observe your own reactions to people from the diversity culture. Be specific about the signals that provoke you. For example, "I took one look at her Outback and all her bumper stickers, and I *knew* who I was dealing with."
- Consider whether your reactions are sparked by fear. Do you avoid diversity people or engage them? Do you feel superior? If so, how would you interact with them if you set your superiority aside?
- What are you curious to know about the specific diversity people you meet? How might you satisfy your curiosity?

Part 1

UNDERSTAND THE TENSION

1

STORIES FROM NEW YORK, FRISCO, AND SYCHAR

The *New York Times* on the Web is full of status signals. Its ads are for art films, exotic travel, and luxury goods. The *Times* is a strong brand itself. Its editorial page has been the avatar of mainstream liberalism for decades, and these days its reporting is increasingly partisan. Such status signals say, "This is the Web site for wealthy, well-educated, progressive leaders."

These signals are not merely decorative. The online readership of the *Times* is disproportionately influential and affluent. According to a study by the Consumer Insight Group in 2008, 71.2 percent of the weekday readers are college graduates, and 48.3 percent are in professional/managerial positions, with another 19 percent in senior management positions. Their median household income is $105,415.[1] Their jobs give them direct influence over society's operations day-to-day. They are executives, lawyers, doctors, teachers, and engineers. But they influence others even when they're not at work. They lead society in how they spend money.

This readership can serve as an informal sampling of the diversity culture's upper class. What do people in this select group think? What upsets them? What are they curious about?

The *Times* allows us a peek, maintaining a list of its top ten most e-mailed articles. Consider one story that appeared on that list. Sydney McGee, a popular art teacher, was suspended from her job after leading eighty-nine fifth-graders through a museum. The children saw nudes.

When a story like this hits the media, our woman at Café Siddhartha chooses a side prejudicially. She doesn't have to know anything about McGee, her teaching techniques, or the specific nude pieces the children saw. She doesn't have to know anything about McGee's relations with administrators, colleagues, or parents. She simply sees the headline of Ralph Blumenthal's article about McGee for the *New York Times*, "Museum Field Trip Deemed Too Revealing," and knows exactly what it's about.[2]

Our Reagan-red Baptist also takes a side automatically. He doesn't have to know what sort of family life the children have, what sort of values their parents display, what sort of relationship the parents have cultivated with the school or with McGee. He just knows what this incident means.

Why do people react so quickly on the basis of so little?

When we gather at contemporary wells, our heads are full of stories, and we use those stories to interpret people. *Who is that woman? What is her agenda? How does she view herself in this situation?* We're also sensitive to the stories others use to interpret us. *Who does that woman think I am? What does she expect my agenda to be? How does she view herself in relation to me?* The answers to such questions come from our stories about subcultures, regions, and status. And the stories are compelling. They often replace interaction.

The first barrier between evangelicals and the diversity culture is built of narratives told over and over—especially by the media. Evangelicals have stories about Café Siddhartha and the café has stories about evangelicals. To cross this barrier, evangelicals will need another story to interpret the people of the diversity culture.

Probe Blumenthal's article with a *Times* reader's eyes. See why it jumped onto the most e-mailed list when it was published on September 30, 2006, and why it remained there several days. The suspension of Sydney McGee fit one of the *Times* readership's well-developed narratives.

Start with the dateline—Frisco, Texas.

Texas is the land of large egos in large bodies living on large ranches. Read the name "Frisco" and you hear the spurs.

Move to the article's accompanying photograph. McGee, 51, stands in contemplation amid the white walls of the Dallas Museum of Art. Her blonde hair is beautifully coiffed and she is well-tailored. The fabric she wears is lively but not daring, her jewelry not gaudy. She is framed by two paintings on the wall behind her, two Mondrians.

The Liberal Arts: Seven classical disciplines spanning language, science, and aesthetics that give intellectual, not vocational, training.

This, *Times* reader, speaks to your liberal arts information. Piet Mondrian (1872–1944) was a Dutch painter regarded as the "most radical abstractionist of our time."[3] His paintings often bore titles like, "Composition with Yellow, Blue, and Red" (1921). Looking at his arrangement of squares and rectangles on the canvas, you admire the equilibrium of his design— the balance of large shapes versus small—and the intuitive way Mondrian found this balance. When his titles are more expressive, like "Broadway Boogie Woogie" (1942–43), you're still looking at colored squares and rectangles. But you're making associations with jazz, and you like that the associations aren't spelled out. Paul Johnson writes of Mondrian, "Once engaged in his abstract experiments, he never abandoned them but kept himself pure from nature (as he saw it)."[4] The message of the photograph is precise: here is a lovely woman, a paragon of diversity, deeply cultivated, and fluent in the arcane language of modern art. She doesn't just know what Mondrians are; she likes them.

Not the person you, *Times* reader, expect to swagger out of Frisco. But Blumenthal sets you straight about the town. In his lead, he describes Frisco as a "moneyed boomtown that is gobbling up the farm fields north of Dallas."

"Moneyed" to you means upscale exurban. The landscape has become an environmental and aesthetic disgrace. The farmland is not merely "gobbled up"; it's now a paved canyon of big box stores. Cars brood at stoplights by the thousands. The air is toxic.

"Boomtown" here connotes both the stereotypical Frisco—the Old West of it—and the crass Frisco—what exurban money builds and buys. Everything is new, gleaming with prosperity—Lincoln Navigators purring past Nordstrom and Applebee's. "Nearly two dozen new schools have been built in the last decade and computers outnumber students three to one." Blumenthal hasn't forgotten the churches, the big box churches with acres of parking. He knows you'll supply those in your mental picture.

So you get it. Frisco looks like Fresno, California, that exurban sprawl you drove through once. In fact, it is Fresno: it's a Fresno theme-park in Texas. They don't swagger after all. They roar out in Hummers. If they ever tour art museums, their glum teenagers are iPodded, longing to go back to Abercrombie or wherever. And no, they don't ever tour art museums. In Frisco-Fresno, they think a Mondrian is a native of Mondria.

Sydney's trapped in one of those places.

Enter two school administrators, a parent, and an anonymous child.

When Sydney took the fifth-graders through the Dallas Museum of Art, everyone agrees, the children saw nudes here and there. The anonymous child complained to the parent—and you just know she's an evangelical from a big box church trying to work her agenda—who frightened the administrators with lawyers. The administrators suspended Sydney with pay and then announced they wouldn't renew her contract. Typical.

Note Blumenthal's account of the petty details: as a *Times* reader, you react to the administrators' confident ignorance.

The administrators don't get out much. They complain about McGee's wearing "flip-flops" to work, when Sydney was wearing sandals by Via Spiga. Flip-flops! They thought Via Spiga sandals were flip-flops!

The administrators have no artistic values. The route along which the fifth-graders were herded featured "the marble torso of a Greek youth . . . circa 330 B.C.," Auguste Rodin's "Shade," and Jean Arp's "Star in a Dream." Neither the principal nor the superintendent would say which work was offensive, referring only to "an abstract nude sculpture." Like an abstract nude is pornographic!

The parent and the administrators are prigs. Sydney said she previewed the tour to ensure the children saw nothing inappropriate. The museum director, John R. Lane, said, "I think you can walk into the Dallas Museum of Art and see nothing that would cause concern." The teachers union representative said this incident was "the first 'nudity-in-a-museum case' we have seen." Dallas-area TV stations indulged visual sarcasm by showing "images of statues from the museum with areas of the anatomy blacked out."

Exactly.

In your eyes, *Times* reader, abiding by sexual restrictions is a sign of backwardness, insularity, and arrested development.

The woman at Café Siddhartha just knows: this is a story about pavement prigs frightened by art. Blumenthal's article closes with quotes from a parent about Sydney's suspension: "I thought she was the greatest . . . [but] knowing Texas, the way things work here . . . I wasn't really amazed. I was like, 'Yeah, right.'"

Ancient Prejudice

The Samaritan woman and Jesus approached the well with stories about each other. What were their stories?

Primary sources of Samaritan history are few, so learning the exact narrative she had for interpreting a Jewish rabbi is impossible. But ancient sources do comment on the conflict between Samaritans and Jews, and some reconstruction of her point of view may be useful. The stories of John Hyrcanus, after all, were etched into Sychar's very landscape.

Stand in Samaritan shoes. Consider the ancient Jewish historian Josephus and his partisan classic, *The Antiquities of the Jews*.[5] Watch how he describes the slowly intensifying Samaritan-Jewish conflict.

Here, for instance, is Josephus's story of how you Samaritans originated.

Cutheans were resettled into Samaria after the conquest of Israel by Assyria. The Cutheans "brought their own gods into Samaria, and by worshipping them, as was the custom of their own countries, they provoked Almighty God to be angry and displeased at them." A plague came on the Samaritans "and when they found no cure for their miseries, they learned by oracle that they ought to worship Almighty God, as the method for their deliverance." They asked the Assyrian king to send them an Israelite priest. Once taught "the holy worship of God, they worshipped him in a respectful manner, and the plague ceased immediately." Josephus notes that "they continue to make use of the very same customs to this very time."[6]

Maybe you like this recounting of your history, Samaritan reader. Maybe you just tolerate it. But you won't like Josephus's next comment, encapsulating his story of what Samaritans were all about:

> And when they see the Jews in prosperity, they pretend that they are changed, and allied to them, and call them kinsmen, as though they were derived from Joseph, and had by that means an original alliance with them: but when they see them falling into a low condition, they say they are no way related to them, and that the Jews have no right to expect any kindness or marks of kindred from them, but they declare that they are sojourners that come from other countries.[7]

He just called you a cynical liar. He just said, "You can't trust those Samaritan tales. The Samaritans are all about politics."

If you keep reading—admittedly a big *if*—you find Josephus has planted the plague story and his bitter comment for later use. The story sets perspective when he tells how the returned Israelite exiles from Babylon reconstructed the Jerusalem temple.

In a public celebration of the new temple, the Levites sang hymns and blew their trumpets, while the elders recalled the former temple's demolished glory. "The wailing of the old men, and of the priests, on account of the deficiency of this temple . . . overcame the sounds of the trumpets and the rejoicing of the people."[8]

The Samaritan people, Josephus reports, heard this sound and "came running together, and desired to know what was the occasion of this tumult." Learning it was connected to the temple construction, they went to Zerubbabel and the Jewish leaders "and desired that they would give them leave to build the temple with them, and to be partners with them in building it."[9]

The Samaritans expressed themselves this way: "We worship their God, and especially pray to him, and are desirous of [the Israelites'] religious settlement, and this ever since Shalmanezer, the king of Assyria, transplanted us out of Cuthah and Media to this place."[10] Josephus shows them referring to their hard lesson under the plague: they learned to "pray especially" to the true God after suffering his wrath and by hearing from a Jewish priest how to worship the right way. You Samaritans were sucking up because the Jews were prospering.

The Samaritan claim was rebuffed. Zerubbabel and the other leaders, wise to your Samaritan scheming, replied "that it was impossible for them to permit them to be their partners, whilst they [only] had been appointed to build that temple at first by Cyrus, and now by Darius." But the Samaritans could come worship in Jerusalem like all the other nations.[11]

As far as you are concerned, Samaritan reader, Josephus has just slandered your piety. Your forefathers repented of their idolatry sincerely, but the Jews reject you because you are a threat to their power. "The Israelite temple wasn't about the true worship of God. We know as much about holiness as the Jews. They just want to control the land from Jerusalem. That temple is about politics."

Stories like these clearly influenced the Samaritan woman's interpretation of Jesus. She was suspicious of him from the start of the conversation, asking, "How is it that You, being a Jew, ask me for a drink since I am a Samaritan woman?" (John 4:9). She asserted ownership of the well, saying Jacob himself had given it to her people through Joseph (4:5, 12). And the controversy about Jerusalem and Gerizim played a significant role in the dialogue. "Our fathers worshiped in this mountain, but you people say that in Jerusalem is the place where men ought to worship" (4:20). Political stories guided her maneuvering with the rabbi.

But Jesus did not have a story about Samaritans to match.

He interpreted the woman at the well with a story that had nothing to do with Jewish-Samaritan conflicts. To begin with, his story about her allowed him to share her cup (4:7). He also interpreted her as being eligible for "the gift of God," the "living water" (4:10). Jesus' story about the woman allowed him to talk with her, probably alone, even though she was five times divorced and living in an immoral relationship (4:18).

To be more specific, Jesus asked all of the same questions that we ask when we meet someone new. *Who is that woman? What is her agenda? How does she view herself in this situation?* He asked the same questions about what the woman thought of him. *Who does that woman think I am? What does she expect my agenda to be? How does she view herself in relation to me?* But his answers were not like ours. We interpret people as stock characters, as members of groups. Jesus interpreted the woman at the well using a story about her as an individual.

Individual: A single person, distinct from a group of people, created in God's image (Psalm 139).

That story enabled him to overcome barriers, and it will do the same for us.

The Baptist at the Well

Our Reagan-red Baptist at Café Siddhartha has a choice.

A woman across the room is half turned away, staring at the vacant chair next to him with the edge of her mouth tugged to one side. Her eyes drop when they meet his. Her shoulders are rigid, and her elbow tightens over her big leather portfolio as she picks a path through the tables. She wants the chair over which he has draped his arm.

What story will he use to interpret her?

Maybe he sees the portfolio and thinks, "Art teacher. She's one of the elites who use the public schools to corrupt children's imaginations and morals. She's like that crazy woman from Texas they were talking about a couple years ago on the radio. Taking fifth-graders to see nudes in a museum! There are so many more things the kids could look at besides naked women. At least in Texas the school administrators have some guts. Not here in California; the administrators would brag about the trip just to prove how open they are."

But we also have a choice of stories for interpreting the Baptist.

Maybe there's more to him than his dark blue suit. Maybe he ignores the leather portfolio. Possibly he knows a story about the woman that permits him to interpret her as an individual—even though she may not show him the same consideration. If so, he can overcome her stories about him. Where she is rigid, he can be flexible. Where her comments are reactive, his can be thoughtful. He can be far ahead of her in perceiving the true significance of their interactions, and can make comments that heal.

But before we consider what his alternative story for the woman might be, we have to ask why that leather portfolio is so provocative.

BECOMING A HEALER: CROSS THE BARRIER OF STORIES

- Watch your favorite news program, or visit your favorite news Web site. Observe your reactions to the stories, especially your prejudices about people. Do you assume information about them that is not in the reports? What triggers those assumptions?
- Do the producers and writers encourage you to rely on your prejudices in making judgments about their stories? In what ways?
- How would you interpret strangers if you never watched the news?

2

PERSONAL IDENTITY ON SATURDAY

His book is thick, close to Norman Mailer tonnage. Rimless glasses sit on his nose, but he's not reading. The book, open to about page nine, is his excuse to lounge in the local independent coffee shop and meditate.

His hair is gray and thinning, longish over his neck, and he has combed it back in fine rows on this Saturday morning. His full beard is trimmed. Over a charcoal long-sleeved T-shirt he has buttoned a black wool vest—all the way to the top. His unfaded jeans are rolled up twice in neat cuffs to crown his polished hiking shoes.

On a fleshy finger is a wedding ring, directing attention to his wife, who sits next to him filling out evaluation forms. She has her rimless glasses, her wedding ring, her dark T-shirt and walking shoes, and her salt-and-pepper hair.

With mochas mostly drained before them, the couple seems straightforward. We have two white, thoughtful establishment people—likely educational establishment, likely connected to the university three blocks away. And here they are in the adagio movement of their weekly cycle.

They seem straightforward, that is, until they get up to leave.

He slides his book into a bag, hoists the shoulder strap over his head and across his vest, and pats the bag when it rests on his hip. We stare at this bag because it's turquoise—loud Native American turquoise—with elaborate patterns woven in white and red, and with fringes dangling off the flap.

How do we interpret the bag? Did our sedate establishment guy make an impulse purchase at the pueblo?

He catches us staring and drills us through his spectacles. *Thought you had me pegged, didn't you? Thought you had me in the right box. Well now you know: they haven't manufactured a box shaped like me yet. Deal with it.*

Chastened, we realize that his persona makes better sense. There was something about the longish hair, something about the look in his eye, something even about the little glasses that exuded '60s counterculture. The vest was another tip: an offbeat affectation. And his wife's hair: we realize that she hasn't changed it since she was nineteen. It's straight and flows to her waist. No clips, no sprays, and definitely no color weave. She has a blessed freedom from middle class beauty aids.

So what if he's a neatnik. Once, he was a tidy hippy.

Now we look around the coffee shop and realize that mixed signals are everywhere.

There's another middle-aged white guy with olive, flat-front chinos—pressed, worn at his waist not his hips—paired with a burgundy button-down. This conventionality is teased by longish hair and more Native American handicraft—a woven belt. He's with a woman roughly his own age who leans in to talk to him. Like the bookster's wife who just left, she has aged without any help from Maybelline, and nobody will criticize.

But they have no wedding rings. *Yeah we're together, but don't read too much into it. The white picket fence never held any appeal for us.*

Yonder is a couple with a one-year-old. Over his slumped shoulders, dad wears a red T-shirt that bulges at his belly. He adjusts his rectangular glasses under a Nike cap and sets the stroller brake with the toe of his Converse. So far, so dad. But then we notice that his jeans slide down to reveal his briefs. White dad in the hood? For her part, mom is rail-thin in jeans that are tight at the hips and boot-cut at the ankles. Her light blue blouse is buttoned exactly twice, but fear not: there's a three-quarter sleeve T-shirt. While she spoons food into baby, her sunglasses perch on top of her black glossy hair.

Don't misinterpret the kid; we're still hot.

Now a Latina takes her seat. Everything from the animal print slip-ons to the shirt unbuttoned, as Tom Wolfe might say, down to *there*, to the short, black hair with blond highlights on the bangs advertises her freedom. An older, white man in this mid-size California town might wonder when her parents "came to this country." But her language is central valley cool. Her hoodie is green and yellow with beads, and on the back is emblazoned, "American Rock & Royalty."

She grew up here, and she's not as available as she seems: there's a big diamond on her wedding ring.

Across the street, emerging from a dark green, late-model Volvo, is movie-star handsome guy—and his olive complexion is only the beginning. He is young and his shirt is loosely buttoned and untucked. His black hair waves above stark features, animated by eyes that probe. He crosses the street in an easy stride, and enters the café with a charisma that keeps women of all ages glued to his movements.

The waitress greets him by name—and with a certain glow on her face. When he orders, she leans in because he speaks low. While he waits at the counter for his latte, he greets two or three other people with a quick nod from the chin.

Waiting for him at a corner table is an Indonesian woman in a peach track suit and white Reeboks, whose hair is streaked with gray. She emits signals of subdued prosperity from the style and quality of her makeup, and from the cut and sheen of her hair. An aged white man in a light blue cardigan shuffles to her table, braces his hand on the back of a chair, and lowers himself next to her. She is attentive to him, and he is attentive to his newspaper. He's waiting for Dark and Handsome too.

Mr. Charisma glides with his latte to the pair, slips into his seat, looks at the old man and says, "Father."

Not *Dad. Father.* We're in the presence of a deeply traditional household.

Into this collection of people at the coffee shop walks perfection, slender with posture that just won't quit. Her years are discretely managed by the beauty aids foresworn by others. Her short brown hair is painstakingly casual. The sleeves of her black cashmere turtleneck are pushed up past the wrists. Her jewelry is fine: a gold watch, and long, black, dangling earrings. As part of this presentation, somehow, her animal print bag merely raises her cute-quotient.

No mixed signals, no irony, no defensiveness—except perhaps in the way she studies the others out of the corners of her eyes. Simply put, she'll be in church tomorrow.

Mixed signals form a second barrier between the diversity culture and evangelicals—the more intimidating because the signals are often part of a strategy. People wear and carry objects that feed stories about who they are, how they see themselves, and what their agendas are. Sometimes the mixed signals are calculated and even defensive, but in other cases they simply reflect the bearer's experiences—and evangelicals can have trouble discerning which. These improbabilities and complexities can make interaction seem pointless.

The Invented Self

We may gain insight from a contrast: we don't find fashion ironies in older generations.

Take Mr. Charisma's father, the old man in the cardigan. It doesn't occur to men of the World War II generation to mix their status symbols. **Irony**: The quality of being contradictory or improbable.

A white, Midwestern man from that era will keep his bushes trimmed and the paint on his house fresh. His Sears pants will be mated with a certain species of plaid shirt. His hair will be short, short, short on the neck and slicked back. His only concession to the times was granted years ago: he abandoned Brylcreem.

And why is he so uncomplicated?

Because he knows who he is. He grew up at a time of strong localities, less mobility between states or even towns, and sharper distinctions

between classes and races—all which tended to make him, if not necessarily bigoted, narrow. His time spent with media was limited (though increasing). This man has never felt the need to carve out a place for himself
in society; his place was inherited.

His ethnic identifications remain strong. If he grew up Italian in Man-
hattan, Polish in Chicago, or (like my grandparents) Danish in Nebraska,
he always thinks of himself as a son of immigrants. The folkways, the language, the priorities of the old country still command his emotions. If he
grew up African-American in the District of Columbia, Irish in Boston, or
Latino in Los Angeles, the story of his people's struggle and success in the
midst of a bigoted culture reinforces his identity.

The World War II man also thinks of himself in terms of the region he
is from: Tennessee, New Jersey, Iowa. Because his accent and daily habits
predate television, they were received from the community around him.
Even his diet remains regional.

A career of fifty years isn't powerful enough to change his fundamental
self-concept. If his father was a farmer, he thinks of himself as a farm kid
even though he became an aerospace engineer. If his father was an urban
grocer, he still thinks of himself as living above the store even though he
became a professor.

The man of World War II has something increasingly rare: an authentic
culture. His inherited identity gives him a confidence in relation to others
that is almost aristocratic.

For many reasons, this man's son did not inherit the same strong place
in society from him. Partly because of the society World War II Man built,
the son grew up at a time when ethnic segregation was being challenged,
and racial distinctions were being reinterpreted. Mobility not only across
the United States but across the globe was increasing. And the American
consumer society with its profuse entertainments was wearing away local
cultures with the power of new media. The son grew up breathing a different atmosphere from his father, less focused on cultural distinctions than
on the softening influences of cultural interaction.

Now, with all these forces greatly intensified, few people in America inherit a sharp personal identity from their culture. Instead, the consumer society requires them to invent themselves.

Many now grow up not knowing who they are.

The woman of Café Siddhartha grew up in a suburb in California's central valley—a town you can find in many places. Her father's jobs—he had several, from sales to management to consulting—provided no particular way of life for her. Indeed, she was disconnected from what he did every day. Her time was spent going to school, watching television, and listening to Top 40, so much of her cultural information came from her peers, not from the adults around her.

So in the diversity culture, an item such as the woman's leather art portfolio is not just functional, doesn't merely protect her drawings from the weather. The portfolio announces a claim. "I design visual beauty." This claim helps define who she is. It announces part of her invented self.

In one sense, the invented self is neither good nor bad. There is nothing right or wrong, godly or ungodly in creating an identity that expresses who you are in a changing, highly interactive society. But a fluid identity has a downside.

The Narcissistic Self

Consider the recent darling of the consumer society, Starbucks. The chain is about more than coffee. It's designed to earn millions by mirroring the customer's self-concept. In October, 2006, Susan Dominus wrote a Sunday *New York Times* piece, "The Starbucks Aesthetic," documenting how this is done. She writes that "the chain is increasingly positioning itself as a purveyor of premium-blend culture."[1]

Her article spent two days on the *Times* most e-mailed list, suggesting that many in the diversity culture had strong opinions about this corporate strategy.

Dominus shows the emotional power of Starbucks for its core customers, many of whom identify with diversity culture values. She quotes

Herbie Hancock: "Going to Starbucks, you feel kind of hip. I feel kind of hip when I go to Starbucks; that's how I know!" This from a jazz great who presumably doesn't need to help his hipness by going to a store.

Why does Starbucks have this power?

At one level, Starbucks gains its emotional hold by working the classic business paradigm: give customers what they want. Dominus introduces us to Anne Saunders, senior vice president of global brand strategy and communications. "Customers say one of the reasons they come is because they can discover new things—a new coffee from Rwanda, a new food item." If they come to explore, then Starbucks orders up more serendipity. With a label on a bag of beans, it refers to the hours of NPR reports customers have heard about Rwanda and shows some hope.

Dominus quotes one customer on the significance of the merchandise: "Some people of caring hearts and minds have looked at this and felt it was worthwhile and beneficial and would create a good vibe in the world." So the old paradigm still works.

But Starbucks operates at another level—down a couple strata from the business model.

You might think the customer quoted above is a nineteen-year-old garage band drummer, but he's not. Starbucks knows who he is and what he thinks about himself. He is Thomas Hay, a 48-year-old contractor. His age makes him a baby boomer who may have grown up vanilla suburban. His trade makes him down-to-earth—just shoot the nails and git-r-done. But his lingo? The "caring hearts and minds" thing, the "good vibe" thing? The lingo is Hay's mixed signal. He tells us that he's no redneck but a bohemian, a guy who has lived some un-middle class experiences.

With its merchandise and ethos, Starbucks doesn't just give Hay what he wants but mirrors his invented self. The claims he would make about his identity are reflected back by the chain. Dominus comments, "There's the faintest whiff of discriminating good taste around everything Starbucks sells, a range of products designed, on some level, to flatter the buyer's self-regard."

But I find yet a deeper level to this interaction. Customers like Hay seem to respond to Starbucks by releasing dollars with a sort of obedience, as if they were following an authority figure.

Consider the success of the chain's non-coffee offerings such as CDs. A Ray Charles CD sold eight hundred thousand copies at Starbucks alone. That production was a joint venture with Concord Records that won several Grammy Awards. Even when Starbucks sells existing titles from other labels, the chain "is typically responsible for at least 10 percent of overall sales." An old Frank Sinatra album, for instance, increased sales twentyfold when Starbucks stocked it. "Since [Madeleine Peyroux's] album 'Careless Love' started selling at Starbucks, its sales have tripled."

Whatever you say, Starbucks.

Now go really subterra: the chain's attentiveness to customers' invented selves allows it to dialogue with their narcissism.

Nikkole Denson selects the books Starbucks retails, and Dominus shows us some of her criteria. Denson says she wants books that provide "almost an education without being preachy." I think there's a finely tuned concept of learning between those quotation marks, a concept gained from knowing the customer's insecurities.

Narcissism: Desire for oneself, named for the mythical Narcissus who fell in love with his reflection.

"Almost" an education. The customer wants books that educate him without making him feel schooled. He is curious but wouldn't want anyone to think he is pretentious. He sees himself as serious but doesn't want to come across as morbid. For him, learning should just be playing. If Denson were to select books that allowed no sense of play, she would offend the customer in a fundamental way: she would confront him with his curiosity's limits.

But the qualifier "almost" is insufficient. The books should almost educate without being "preachy." Their writing should have humility, a lack of self-righteousness. The authors should be able to distance themselves emotionally from their subjects, so as not to convey any sense of judgment. Starbucks' reflection of the customer's invented self must be rigorously positive.

Drill even deeper.

One of the ways Dominus expresses Starbucks' manipulations is by juxtaposing the word "culture" in her analysis with the word "entertainment" in quotations from executives, as if the two terms were interchangeable. She may be unconscious of the habit, or she may intend it to indict cynicism in the chain's interactions with its customers. Regardless, I believe her pairings of *culture* and *entertainment* reflect how open to manipulation personal identity has become in the consumer society.

For example, go back to her opening thesis that Starbucks wants to purvey "premium-blend culture." To explain the idea, she quotes chairman Howard Schultz: Starbucks wants to expand into "entertainment."

Later, Dominus calls a book by Mitch Albom a new item in Starbucks' "cultural portfolio." Then she gives us back to Schultz, who explains that the company's partnerships enable it "to create an entertainment platform."

In another instance, Dominus quotes executives describing the goal of the company's "cultural extensions": to push the "sense of discovery into entertainment."

To be sure, culture and entertainment are related. But the terms "culture" and "entertainment" are not interchangeable in this manner.

Culture is a way of thought and life. It includes faith, family, work, region, art, and history. World War II Man had culture. Entertainment is what cultures employ as diversion from labors and cares. It can include some forms of art like cinema, literature, theater, and music. The generations after World War II Man came to be focused on entertainment.

My guess is that the diversity culture readers of the *Times* were not of one mind in e-mailing this article. Some passed it on to say, "Starbucks gets it. They know we want to explore." Others said, "Look, another manipulative corporation, another destroyer of authenticity." Many of them are disturbed by corporate empires profiting from the consumer's shifting sense of self. Starbucks both epitomizes and antagonizes the people of diversity.

Here's my hunch: the diversity culture is conflicted about consumerism, neither entirely rejecting nor reconciling with it. Diversity people seek to be free from boxes, while consumerism is about boxing people up. They played a large role in Starbucks' success, but with regrets. They may sense that their culture of openness is not powerful enough to keep its people from being boxed voluntarily.

The Samaritan Self

I believe the Samaritan woman's identity is central to Jesus' interactions with her. Is her sense of self strong?

Consider how the conversation would go if she were an unquestioning, sharply defined Samaritan who felt completely one with the story and ways of her people. If her inherited identity were unsoftened, I think the dialogue in John 4 would be a lot shorter.

That inherited identity has a definite presence. The woman seems to know who she is when she says, "How is it that You, being a Jew, ask me for a drink since I am a Samaritan woman?" (John 4:9). She apparently feels she has a place in her culture, referring to "our father Jacob" who "gave us the well" (4:12). She is expressing confidence that she received Jacob's legacy just like the other citizens of Sychar.

On closer inspection, however, the Samaritan woman's sense of identity is less sharp than it seems, as we can see by observing Jesus' statements and her responses.

Jesus' opening, "Give Me a drink" (4:7), is a trespass on her person as forceful as invading her physical space. Yet she responds with uncertainty (4:9). She does not brush him off, insult him, or ignore him, as any confident Samaritan might be expected to do (Luke 9:52–53). Instead, she asks him a question. She invites Jesus to explain himself. She will listen to him on a subject that ought to be closed.

In opening the conversation this way, Jesus acts as if the Samaritan and Jewish cultures don't exist and she's willing to play along.

Jesus' answer to her question is pushy (4:10). "If you knew the gift of

God, and who it is who says to you, 'Give Me a drink,' you would have asked Him, and He would have given you living water." The pushiness comes from three ways he challenges her cultural assumptions.

First, Jesus claims that she's made a mistake about his identity. Jesus constructs the "if" clause to assume the negative: "If you knew who I am—and you don't—you would ask me for a drink." He is saying that her inherited information about Jews is irrelevant to a conversation about who he is.

Second, Jesus claims that Jews have made a mistake about her identity. Jews from the time of Herod the Great thought Samaritans shouldn't have any access to God. Samaritans were banned from the temple after some of them threw dead bodies into the temple courts during Passover.[2] Jesus, by contrast, says that the woman is ignorant of her access to "the gift of God." She should ignore the hostility that seeks to exclude her from worship.

Third, and perhaps most shocking, Jesus claims she would ask him for the gift, if only she had not inherited falsehoods. If she had understood the irrelevance of the Jewish-Samaritan conflict to Jesus' mission, she would have initiated the conversation herself, and gone right to the point: Give me living water.

Samaritan culture, even in the heat of ethnic and religious hostility, is not powerful enough to keep the woman from listening to Jesus. It's not powerful enough because, in fact, she is not confident of her place in the community. Her identity is softened, and Jesus focuses on this fluidity: he claims to have a prior relationship with her, of which she is ignorant.

Why is the Samaritan woman uncertain of her place?

The reason surfaces late in her conversation with Jesus (4:18). She has had five husbands. She has been divorced at the initiative of every single one, all according to the law of Moses in Deuteronomy 24:1–4.[3] The place of such a woman among the people of God is unclear. Who in the community will call her righteous when the elders and her husbands have called her immoral? Especially when she's just come from the house of her new friend.

Jesus overcomes the woman's second barrier because he knows her identity as a Samaritan has been softened. He uses another story to interpret her, and is now opening to her the possibility of a new sense of self.

The Baptist at the Well

Our Baptist at Café Siddhartha has another choice to make.

He moves his arm off the back of the vacant chair and watches the woman lean her portfolio against the table leg. *She didn't buy that at the Totes outlet. Look at the leather, the stitching around the edge!* His eyes shift to her boots, which gleam at him. *Were they molded to her feet?* His eyes pass but do not linger over the fabric of her trousers. *Whatever it is, it ain't rayon.* His eyes cruise to her face. *She didn't get that tan hanging around here.* And at the edge of her eyebrow, he spots a glint of silver. *Piercing?! At her age?*

She nods at the chair and squints at him. "Thanks."

But, again, we have a choice of stories about the Baptist. He might indeed react to her status symbols. But what if the Baptist has a deep understanding of people? What if, even with his Reagan-red tie, he can bring out this wisdom in relation to the woman? He might, after all, consider the importance of her invented self, not as an expression of her confidence but of her doubts. He might ask to what extent she has effaced a previous identity. He might also know ways that her doubts can be addressed.

But before we can discover some of those ways, we have to understand her street philosophy.

BECOMING A HEALER: CROSS THE BARRIER OF IRONY

- Who in your life do you consider pretentious? Which of their specific characteristics feed your perception? What weaknesses do you think they are covering up?
- How do you guard what you feel are your weaknesses? What specific strategies do you use to make sure others don't penetrate your guard?
- How would you want others to treat your weaknesses if they saw them?

STREET POSTMODERNISM

Postmodernism has been topic A among evangelicals for a couple of decades. Its contours seem well-known by now.

The Enlightenment is over and, with it, the modern age. The rationalism that dominated the seventeenth, eighteenth, and nineteenth centuries was arrogant in its certainty that the Western mind could explain all mysteries and engineer new societies. Logic has no grounding in objective reality, only in metanarratives, the all-encompassing stories that prophesy triumph and justify power grabs. One group's truth is the enemy of everyone else's freedom.

The reactions of many evangelicals to postmodernism are also well-known. Postmodernism subordinates principles to personal experiences. It is relativism by another name, the same old idea that there are no absolutes, the same old enemy of God and truth.

But my summary of these issues is like a satellite image that takes in Asia, Africa, and Australia at a glance. It merely captures a few slogans.

The term *postmodern* has too convoluted a history to summarize so simplistically. The term, after all, was first used to describe a school of architecture. While postmodernism in philosophy is related to postmodernism in literature, the two are still distinct. There is postmodernism in music and film, too, and expressions of it surface in most academic disciplines. A family of terms such as *deconstructionism* and *post-structuralism* has been generated by postmodern influences, but each of the terms has its own history. None of these distinctions shows up in my satellite photograph.

To add another set of complications, the average person in the diversity culture has not studied postmodernism at any depth. Important postmodern thinkers such as Michel Foucault and Jacques Derrida have name recognition in the dilettante mind of the liberal arts. But how many educated people have actually read them? Read more of their work than an essay or two? How many are fluent in the debates among various schools of postmodern thought? Very few, and I am not among them.

The woman at Café Siddhartha, for instance, has not studied deeply beyond her training in art. She may know postmodern painting, but she is unlikely to know postmodern literary criticism. Her ethics could be broadly classified as postmodern, but she is only partly informed by philosophers, and what knowledge she has of them is derived from popularizations. She has synthesized her ethics in the hustle of life, commerce, and love, not in the quiet tension of the academy.

She has a postmodernism of the street. Which is to say, she has a set of attitudes, a satellite image of postmodernity—taken by a different satellite than the one that took mine.

In trying to deal with the most significant cultural shift of our time, therefore, evangelicals are not sure what they face. They aren't sure how the shift affects the individuals they talk to. Nor are they sure what their role should be in relation to those individuals. Should they educate them about postmodernity? (Probably not a wise posture.) Should they try to accommodate their views? (Definitely not wise.) The sheer diversity of attitudes on the street is daunting.

The attitudes of street postmodernism form the third barrier between the diversity culture and evangelicals. This barrier is less a wall than a maze. For evangelicals to pass through, they have to sense which corridors in a person's ethic will lead to open communication on the other side.

Interacting with Bobos

Today's street postmodernism is another form of the street philosophies that people develop in every age. And what do I mean by street philosophy?

It's an ethic developed by living, not by studying. As a set of attitudes, it doesn't strive for theoretical consistency, or even clarity. Rather, a street philosophy helps an individual to navigate ambiguity. It is not an abstract construct at all, but a social one designed to enable safe, successful interactions where the turf is uncertain.

> **Street Postmodernism**: A set of attitudes that enables a person to navigate today's social ambiguity without getting hurt.

To help us see the street philosophy evangelicals face in the diversity culture, we call upon David Brooks, the conservative *New York Times* columnist. His book, *Bobos in Paradise*, to which I am indebted in this chapter, can help us discern how postmodern attitudes have developed over the past few decades.

Start with a cultural contradiction in terms.

Brooks coined *bourgeois bohemians*, or *Bobos*, to describe what he calls the "new upper class"—a large population of highly educated people who combine values that, in the 1950s and 1960s, were incompatible. Here is how he describes the old value categories:

> The bourgeoisie were the square, practical ones. They defended tradition and middle-class morality. They worked for corporations, lived in suburbs, and went to church. Meanwhile, the bohemians were the free spirits who flouted convention. They were the artists and the intellectuals—the hippies and the Beats. In the old schema the bohemians championed the values of the radical 1960s and the bourgeois were the enterprising yuppies of the 1980s.[1]

Brooks shows that the new upper class combines "the countercultural six-
ties and the achieving eighties into one social ethos."[2]

How did Bobos arrive at this strange mix?

Starting in the 1960s, many baby boomers embraced the bohemian ideal
of freedom from moral standards, exploring all manner of spiritual teachings from Taoism to Silva Mind Control. But in the course of living, they
learned that spirituality needs the limitations they chafed against when
they were younger. The bourgeois realities of raising children gave them
an appreciation of rituals. "Organized religions have a set of stable ceremo-
nies to guide and cultivate the spiritual lives of kids. Self religions do not."[3]
They learned "that freedom and choice aren't everything. Free spirituality
can lead to lazy spirituality, religiosity masquerading as religion, and finally to the narcissism of the New Age movement."[4]

So Bobos are searching for a past. They move to small towns. They
furnish their homes with evocations of the agrarian life, old rituals, and
simpler times. They vacation in "premeritocratic enclaves where the local peasantry live stable, traditional lives." With some poignancy, Brooks
calls Bobos "spiritual reactionaries. They spend much of their time pining
for simpler ways of living, looking backward for the wisdom that people
with settled lives seem to possess but which the peripatetic, opportunity-
grasping Bobos seem to lack." They go, for instance, to Montana "looking
for a place to call home."[5]

Montana's attraction to the bohemian part of Bobos is easy to understand. "After all, the Montana mindset has always celebrated flexibility,
freedom, and independence. This is a state that until recently didn't have
speed limits on its highways, so suspicious are the locals about any authority
telling them how to lead their lives." Still, Montana is not "Marin County
with a timberline." Bobos are also attracted to it as a place for the thick-
skinned. "Native and wannabe native Montanans define themselves against
people who don't have real manure on their boots, who haven't been kicked
a few times by a horse, who haven't stuck around the state long enough to
be painfully lonely."[6]

Montana has something for the Bobo's inner bourgeois too: it has churches. Brooks introduces us to the Rabbi of the only Jewish congregation in the state, Gershon Winkler. The Jews who come to his synagogue in Missoula are from coastal urban centers like Los Angeles and New York, so Rabbi Winkler leads a service that doesn't fit easily within the established categories. "He calls his hybrid approach 'Flexidoxy.'"[7] In places like Montana, the Bobos can combine ancient traditions with postmodern freedoms without losing bourgeois respectability.

> **Flexidoxy**: A hybrid spirituality that selects truths to believe rather than submitting to a system of beliefs.

What is Flexidoxy? Brooks notes that Orthodox Judaism is growing, attracting young people who study the Torah in Hebrew and keep the kosher laws. "They are rigorous observers, but they also pick and choose, discarding those ancient rules that don't accord with their modern sensibilities—most any rule that restricts the role of women, for example." They also pull back from any implication that Judaism is true exclusively and that all other faiths are false. "This is Orthodoxy without obedience— indeed, Flexidoxy."[8]

Flexidoxy is how Bobos reconcile their conservatism with the autonomy they continue to want. Flexidoxy is a street philosophy. It's individualized. Bobos did not form it by studying philosophers or theologians formally, but by synthesizing ideals from a variety of influences—films, novels they read in college, teachers—with the demands of daily living. It is not coherent. It is the sum of their experiences and influences.

Bobos' Flexidoxy fulfills an essential function of a street philosophy: it helps them check how someone interacts with them. Bobo spirituality, Brooks says, "is more of a temperament than a creed."[9] When they hear a new point of view, Bobos will not test its logic, as if they were applying a doctrine. Instead, they will test the messenger, trying to discover if he or she is congenial to Bobo ways. If the messenger's temperament passes, Bobos will pursue the dialogue.

Brooks gives some general guides to the Flexidoxy maze, which I summarize here not to endorse but to highlight. I'll give some evaluation of these guides in chapter 8.

Don't be certain. Bobos are "suspicious of vehemence." Civility is one of their prized virtues. "Bobos are epistemologically modest, believing that no one can know the full truth and so it's best to try to communicate across disagreements and find some common ground."[10]

Don't be a hero. "Bobo moralists are not heroic, but they are responsible. They prefer the familiar to the unknown, the concrete to the abstract, the modest to the ardent. . . ." He cites sociologist Alan Wolfe's finding that the suburban middle class holds a "small scale morality"—an ethic that focuses on specific situations, not abstract principles. "They think of establishing moral relationships with those close to them but do not worry about formal moral rules for all mankind."[11]

Don't be a critic. Bobos enjoy "theological discussions, so long as they are full of praise rather than blame." They value people's good intentions, and are unwilling to criticize what they don't fully understand. "In short, they prefer a moral style that doesn't shake things up, but that protects the status quo where it is good, and gently tries to forgive and reform the things that are not so good."[12]

Evangelicals may be tempted to think they already understand these guidelines.

But Brooks's description of how the generation of the 1960s modified parts of its worldview is at odds with the evangelical story on that group. Most evangelicals have missed the reactionary impulse of maturing baby boomers, thinking of them as if they still wanted to dance in the mud at Woodstock. Evangelicals miss the fact that life gave the boomers a taste for discipline.

Nor is the evangelical story on Flexidoxy reliable. Evangelicals know Flexidoxy as relativism—a toxin from the academy, the public education system, and the entertainment industry. There is no right or wrong. There are no absolutes. And the lusty populace has swallowed the toxin because it's so yummy.

Relativism: The belief that there is no truth.

The real story is not that simple. The people Brooks describes know perfectly well that right and wrong exist. What they don't necessarily know is how to integrate unchanging principles into lives that are full of change. And I see a lot of evangelicals struggling with that conundrum too, and failing with one extreme of solutions or another.

Brooks himself, while sympathetic to Flexidoxy, is critical of its fruits. "Some days I look around and I think we have been able to achieve these reconciliations only by making ourselves more superficial, by simply ignoring the deeper thoughts and highest ideals that would torture us if we actually stopped to measure ourselves according to them." He concludes, with perfectly pitched Bobo irony, "This is a good morality for building a decent society, but maybe not one for people interested in things in the next world, like eternal salvation, for example."[13]

Evangelicals, then, need a story on street postmodernism that accounts for its hopes as well as its failings. Many street postmodernist attitudes are inconsistent with following Christ. But even those often express yearnings for personal depth and integrity that evangelicals are able to address—if they will set aside their satellite photographs and deal directly with the individuals in front of them.

A Samaritan Street Philosophy

Our perception of the relationship between Jews and Samaritans in Jesus' time tends to be black and white. Jews hated Samaritans and vice versa. Neither wanted anything to do with the other.

This perception could use some color.

In the last chapter we showed that the Samaritan woman's identity was fluid, and that Jesus weakened her connection to her community. We said that Jesus acted as if the Samaritan and Jewish cultures didn't exist, and she was willing to play along. *How* she played along can show us more about her attitudes. She was open to Jesus not just because her personal identity was fluid, but also because she seems to have formed a street philosophy that allowed her to explore—carefully, step-by-step—the maze of a rabbi's attitudes.[14]

* * *

She set her eyes on the water jar, watching it descend into the darkness of the shaft, and ignoring the Galilean rabbi sitting on the well. But the ends of his fingers reached into her sight, and he said, "Give me a drink."

Her fists froze on the rope, and her pupils flashed a glance at the fringes on his robe—but only a glance. She pulled her eyes back to the jar and forced her arms to pull the rope again. *Are you insulting me? Or are you up to something worse? Is it even possible that you mean what you say? You get one chance. I'll take this one step into your maze. Only one.* With her eyes fixed on the jar, she replied, "How is it that you, being a Jew, ask me for a drink since I am a Samaritan woman?"

The rabbi withdrew his hand and said, "If you knew the gift of God, and who it is who says to you, 'Give me a drink,' you would have asked him, and he would have given you living water."

She took a breath. *Metaphor. The rabbi's lured me into a metaphor, and he wants to teach me. But what could he possibly have to say? Do I have to remind him that our communities don't get along, that we had a temple on the mountain and a Jew razed it—just for starters? Who does he think he is? Who does he think I am? I'll see how far this corridor takes me before it dead-ends. I can find my way back out.* She looked at his hands and replied, "Sir, you have nothing to draw with and the well is deep; where then do you get that living water? You are not greater than our father Jacob, are you, who gave us the well, and drank of it himself and his sons and his cattle?"

The rabbi's fingers rested on the lip of the shaft. "Everyone who drinks of this water will thirst again; but whoever drinks of the water that I will give him shall never thirst; but the water that I will give him will become in him a well of water springing up to eternal life."

The woman looked at the rabbi's face, and then back to his hands. *No dead end here. The rabbi just answered my question: He thinks he is greater than our father Jacob. A Jew is offering to give me eternal life. It's probably some kind of trick—but why do I not feel threatened? I've got to see where this corridor goes.* She put a little music into her voice and said, "Sir, give me this water, so I will not be thirsty nor come all the way here to draw." Again she looked at his face, inscrutable as any other rabbi's.

He said, "Go, call your husband and come here."

Her breath caught in her throat. *Dead end?*

Interaction Between Samaritans and Jews

If the antagonism between Jews and Samaritans were as black and white as we imagine, then John 4 records nothing less than an interpersonal miracle. But the antagonism was not so stark. While the Jewish and Samaritan cultures did harden from hostility into total rejection, the process of hardening went on for some centuries, and was not yet complete at the time Jesus sat at the contested well.

The generation of Jews at the end of the process is ably represented by Josephus. In his histories, we have already found the antagonism against Samaritans at a vitriolic pitch. Josephus and his generation, which witnessed the destruction of Herod's temple in A.D. 70, would not have tolerated half-breeds.

But Jesus' dialogue with the Samaritan woman took place almost a half-century before. In this generation, while strife between Jews and Samaritans was certainly the norm, it remained full of social ambiguities. It would have been difficult for a Jew and a Samaritan to navigate the maze of each other's hostile ethics—but not impossible.

In order to understand why the woman even took one step into Jesus' maze, we have to look past the stark bigotry of one generation and discover the ambiguous bigotry of another. The Samaritan woman's culture was more diverse than we may realize.

Even in Josephus's accounts there are indications of significant social and religious interactions between the two groups. For instance, Josephus notes that while the temple on Gerizim still stood, Samaritan culture served as a kind of refuge for excommunicated Jews: "If any one were accused by those of Jerusalem of having eaten things common, or of having broken the Sabbath, or of any other crime of the like nature, he fled away to the Shechemites [another of Josephus's names for the Samaritans], and said that he was accused unjustly."[15]

Some Jews, then, when they were disgraced, saw Samaritan religion as an acceptable corner in which to remain under God's covenantal roof. Their numbers were significant enough for Josephus to include the practice of fleeing to Mt. Gerizim in his narrative. To be sure, the practice would not have endeared the alternative priesthood to the Levites, but at least in the populace it does indicate a murky sense of kinship. The permanent settlement of some Jewish families in Samaria, intermarriage with Samaritans, and a further syncretism of ritual practices would have been probable results of this mixture.

The grudgingly shared culture extended even to the temple in Jerusalem. Samaritans were allowed to worship there, at least during the major feasts, into the time of Herod. A single incident changed the policy. Josephus says that during one Passover, when the priests customarily opened the temple gates just after midnight, "some of the Samaritans came privately into Jerusalem, and threw about dead men's bodies in the cloisters; on account of which the Jews afterwards excluded them out of the temple."[16]

This escalation of hostility was relatively recent when Jesus was at Jacob's well. In the longer perspective, the exclusion of the Samaritans from worship was new.

References to the Samaritans in the Talmud show how complex the interactions between the two cultures were in the intertestamental period. James A. Montgomery, in his well-known study of Samaritan history, has documented how fine distinctions became when Samaritans were the subject of rabbinical debate. He summarizes, "Contemporary doctors of the Law hotly dispute over the status of the Samaritans, and changes of opinions on the part of rabbis are recorded."[17]

The Talmud contains some broad vindications of Samaritan purity that are startling to read today. One commendation says, "Every law which the Samaritans have accepted, they are more punctilious in observing than the Jews."[18] Another says flatly that "the land of Samaria is clean."[19]

But on specific issues, the rabbis were more contentious. In contrast to the approving statements above, there is the famous reservation about Samaritans, "This is the rule: Whatever they are suspected in, they are not to be believed in."[20] The rabbis debated questions of ritual, including whether a Samaritan could circumcise a Jewish baby boy (disputed), whether a Jew could rent his house to a Samaritan (yes), and whether a Jew could say the "Amen" to a Samaritan's benediction (yes, so long as the Jew could hear every word).[21] That such matters were debated shows a great deal of interaction between the two groups.

The New Testament itself shows that Jews and Samaritans frequently came into contact. In John 4:8, Jesus' disciples go into Sychar to buy food, which was natural considering the Samaritans' strict adherence to Mosaic dietary laws. Nor was this Jesus' only journey through Samaria. In Luke 9:51–56, Jesus travels south from Galilee to Jerusalem, and chooses the route through Samaria again. In fact, whichever route the Jews from Jerusalem might have favored, the one through Samaria seems to have been traditional among Galileans. But their contact with the inhabitants was never free of trouble. In Luke 9, the disciples are enraged by a Samaritan village's refusal of hospitality—to the extreme of proposing an Elijah-like call for fire from heaven.

Indeed, interactions with diverse cultures had characterized the valley of Shechem, where the Sychar of John 4 was located, for centuries. Montgomery describes it as "the junction of the natural routes traversing this hill-country." The north-south road connecting Judah and Galilee was only one of these routes. Another ran northwest to the cities of Samaria and Caesarea. More routes connected Shechem to the Jordan river valley to the east.[22] Sychar was a center of trade.

The woman at the contested well, then, did not come from a community of black and white antagonisms. While the communities of Jews and Samaritans were bigoted against each other, they were like all such communities living side by side, having beaten paths into the cultural landscape by which to navigate the conflicts without getting hurt. Whatever her prejudices, the woman was streetwise about how to interact in neutral ways with Jews—even with a rabbi sitting on her well.

She took life case by case. And Jesus worked with her.

The Baptist at the Well

Our Baptist cannot know the woman at Café Siddhartha by associating her with the stock characters in his stories. He cannot know her by reacting to her leather portfolio. And he cannot know her by oversimplifying her attitudes. If he speaks to her from any of these sources of false certainty, her alienation from him will be irrevocable.

But, again, he may not be as reactive as we think, this Baptist. We may have a story on him that is wrong. He may have developed the self-control to question his default information, and to speak from a posture of confident curiosity. He may sense that if he can understand what she has endured in close relationships, he'll be able to find a way through the maze of her postmodernism—knowing that her postmodernism is uniquely hers and that it is far from settled.

To put the point differently, he may have a mental category called, "Truths She Has Learned from Life—Truths That Really Are True."

BECOMING A HEALER: CROSS THE BARRIER OF STREET PHILOSOPHY

- How can you tell when someone is trying to avoid conflict?
- What are some strategies that you use to show others that a disagreement with you, even a serious one, is safe? How do you earn trust?
- In the past, what were some ways you lost a person's trust during a disagreement?

4

TRUTH OUT OF THE CRUCIBLE

One Monday morning, the woman leaves Café Siddhartha with a half-consumed mocha, ambles through the fog, and trots up a flight of stairs to her studio. She drains her lukewarm mocha to the grounds while watching her computer boot, and then pulls up the *New York Times*. On the most e-mailed list, she spots "Darwin's God" by Robin Marantz Henig, an examination of Darwinian research into the origins of religion, published the previous day.[1] She clicks it.

Looks heavy. Scrolling to the bottom, she sees that the essay sprawls across eleven pages. But the first sentence is too good to ignore. "God has always been a puzzle for Scott Atran."

God has always been a puzzle for her too.

She didn't hate her parents' church in the San Joaquin valley until she was a senior in high school. Before then, she was little Miss Christian, her hair straight as the virgin Mary's, her dress below her knees, nylons on her legs, and shiny flats covering her toes. Truth be told, she bought into the whole organized religion sham, denying the world and following Jesus. And, truth be told, she was sincere. Hard as it is to admit now, more than thirty years later, Jesus was real to her.

Real, that is, until her picture of Jesus shattered.

For one thing, Jesus wasn't real to her pastor, the Mississippi transplant. Shortly after he came to First Baptist of the Valley, he showed up at a swim party given for the youth. He got in the pool, and swam under her and the other girls, grabbing their legs. No one said anything. The pastor was just a big tease. Until people realized that he seduced many of the women he was counseling.

For another thing, Jesus wasn't real to her church friends. They were doing the same drugs, having sex in the same places, and using the same excuses as her friends who didn't go to church. Most of them swung back and forth between guilty weeks of prayer and jaded months of sarcasm. After leaving church permanently, they settled into irony.

She might have been able to put those pieces of her God-puzzle back together.

But when Mom left Dad just before her senior year, the woman realized that Jesus wasn't real to her parents either. Mom wanted freedom, wanted her teaching career back, and a little thing like her daughter's senior year wasn't enough to hold her in a dead marriage. Dad regarded the divorce as proof that some people simply weren't predestined.

There was no putting the puzzle back together after that.

Diving into "Darwin's God," the woman is surprised by the anger she feels at the subject of evolution. All those people in her parents' church who didn't know Jesus sure knew a lot about creationism. Attending seminar after seminar, the woman learned more about skulls and strata and carbon dating than she ever wanted to know. She heard all about the secular humanist war to destroy faith in God, the war in which evolutionists were the shock troops.

So much devastation in their lives, yet they were obsessed with Darwin, as if the emptiness of their religion was his fault.

So the sentence about Atran summons real passion. Here is a scholar on evolution wrestling with his spirituality. Even Dad would have to be impressed. What had Atran experienced that made God a puzzle? Why was he studying the evolutionary origin of religion? Atran, she reads, is a fifty-five-year-old anthropologist at the National Center for Scientific Research in Paris. Not busy enough in France, he holds other academic appointments in Michigan and New York. Atran might have more to offer than a scientific explanation for First Baptist of the Valley.

But as she reads, she keeps hearing Dad's speeches.

Atran does plenty to provoke evangelicals such as her dad just by studying how religion evolved. Dad would know where this line of argument is headed. If evolutionists can explain how we imagined God in the first place, they can dismiss God—the old "faith evolved because we needed a crutch" ploy. The woman hears her dad warming up: "How can that Atran guy explain away all the complexities of creation? How can he look out into space at night and not come to the conclusion that . . . ?"

The provocations get worse. The woman reads that religion doesn't help the evolutionary process.

Take the belief in life after death. Henig quotes Atran's explanation of it: "Even after someone dies and the body demonstrably disintegrates, that person will still exist, will still be able to laugh and cry, to feel pain and joy." Atran thinks this belief "does not appear to be a reasonable evolutionary strategy. . . . Imagine another animal that took injury for health or big for small or fast for slow or dead for alive. It's unlikely that such a species would survive."

That would get her dad throwing flatware across the room. "Why doesn't this smug academic, with his apartment on the Upper West Side where he gives interviews to reporters, with his research and joint appointments, with his conferences and books and articles, go back to France where he belongs?"

But her dad would miss the other side of Scott Atran, the side that the woman of Café Siddhartha understands, along with many other *Times* readers. Atran has a bigger problem than unraveling evolutionary strategies. He's trying to relate to his fellow human beings.

In the '70s, he went on archaeological tours of Israel, where religious commitment and tradition confronted him everywhere he looked. According to Henig, he wondered why people worked "so hard against their preference for logical explanations to maintain two views of the world, the real and the unreal, the intuitive and the counterintuitive."

Later, in the '80s, he did historical research. "I wondered why no society ever survived more than three generations without a religious foundation as its raison d'être."

Now he wonders why atheists cross their fingers during turbulence, why agnostic university students won't put their hands inside a box after he tells them it's a magical African relic, why human beings maintain a "belief in hope beyond reason."

The full opening of Henig's article reads, "God has always been a puzzle for Scott Atran. When he was 10 years old, he scrawled a plaintive message on the wall of his bedroom in Baltimore. 'God exists,' he wrote in black and orange paint, 'or if he doesn't, we're in trouble.'" The woman never wrote such a thought on her bedroom wall when she was ten. She doesn't know what the pieces of his puzzle were. But she understands what it's like when God is a source of conflict instead of confidence.

Atran has endured something, just like I have.

Dad never understood her crisis. He was never even curious. He never engaged her for five minutes about why Christianity had ceased to be an option for her. He was too busy intellectualizing his personal agony. To this day, he just blames her departure from his faith on her rebellious mother. His soul is booby-trapped against threatening intruders like evolutionists and Buddhist daughters.

When she finishes the article about Atran, she thinks of five friends. "They've got to read this." She clicks the button that says "E-mail," and she is not alone. "Darwin's God" is number one on the *Times* most e-mailed list and remains in that slot for days.

Truths Learned from Life

When patrons of Café Siddhartha describe their personal experiences and the lessons they have learned, they are often referring to a

Crucible: A vessel for melting metal.

deep trial, a set of circumstances that caught them and would not let them escape. We describe people as being in a crucible when they suffer in this life-changing way. Years of sexual abuse as a child are a crucible. A divorce that took a man years to finalize, that destroyed him emotionally, that cost him his job, his kids, and his financial security is a crucible. The disintegration of your family and your worldview—of all that you thought would protect you—is a crucible.

A crucible leaves a person with vivid impressions of wrong, like the woman's feeling of her pastor grabbing her legs in a swimming pool. Because she encounters an evil she didn't know existed, her ethics are revolutionized. Granting trust to a pastor, for instance, becomes dangerous, even immoral. Some of the ethics she chooses in the process of being melted down are profoundly wrong, like her embrace of Buddhism. But not all of them. The woman is not wrong to insist that one's life cohere with one's spirituality.

The importance of a crucible is this: it leaves a person with a knowledge of truths that they will never need to hear explained.

When evangelicals hear a diversity culture person tell about a crucible, they tend to respond in one of two ways.

One is to reject what the person has learned and correct her conclusions. Sorry your father sexually abused you, but lesbianism is a perversion of God's design for sexuality. Yes, your father was an elder in the church all the time you were suffering, but that doesn't make Christianity false. Certainly the people closest to you were hypocritical in whitewashing your father's crimes, but that doesn't give you the right to advocate the overthrow of America's Judeo-Christian heritage.

People don't give this "reject-correct" approach a patient hearing anymore.

The other way is to accept the person's experiences and affirm her conclusions. I totally identify with you. I've seen my share of controlling fundamentalists. You're right, their so-called high standards are just a cover for abuse. But that kind of Christianity is so over. Jesus is way bigger than morality and bigotry and patriarchal privilege.

This "accept-affirm" approach avoids making a futile assault on a person's vivid experiences, but makes the opposite error of approving them indiscriminately.

The fourth barrier between evangelicals and the diversity culture is the inability of evangelicals to engage people wisely.

Some evangelicals seem to believe that a non-Christian can't learn truth from life. All the while they hear the story of someone's crucible, they formulate The Answer, trying to think of a nice way to tell him that he's badly off track. So their attempts to engage the poor, darkened heathen are patronizing. Other evangelicals seem to accept a non-Christian's crucible as automatically legitimate and are so anxious to avoid being judgmental that they abandon the language of sin and righteousness.

> **Engagement**: The act of connecting more deeply with others.

Both factions are missing spectacular opportunities. The truths people learn from life require no evidence, no pleading, and no explanation. People have already paid dearly to learn them. In order to take these opportunities, evangelicals simply need to cross the fourth barrier.

And Jesus has shown us the model of wise engagement.

Truths Learned from a Samaritan Life

What we know about the Samaritan woman's life experience is brief, and our story about her tends to be simplistic.

We know that she was five times divorced, and that when Jesus mentioned her husband, she turned cagey (4:16–18). So our story about her is that she had alienated five husbands with her immorality and was now so hardened that she lived in fornication without any pretence of marriage. Jesus brought up her past to confront her sins.

In this version, Jesus uses the reject-correct approach. The woman is messed up, and she needs to be saved.

I think we should engage the Samaritan woman further. I believe she learned some truths from life that really are true, and there are two reasons from the context of the Gospels why I think so.

To begin with, most of the individuals who appear in the Gospels are sketched. We know nothing about them but the essential details—social position (beggar, synagogue ruler, centurion), race (Jewish, Greek, or Syrophoenician), and relative wealth or poverty (the widow, the tax collector). But in John's gospel, we often get a bit more about the individuals who meet Jesus—enough to start us thinking about their backgrounds.

John gives us the man born blind, for instance, in juxtaposition with his parents (9:1–34), showing their different reactions to the Pharisees' investigations. John shows us the relational dynamic between Jesus and his friends Mary and Martha (11:1–37). John also gives us an extended look at the wavering Roman procurator, Pilate, at the climax of Jesus' trials (18:28–19:22).

Such details, while few, are of a different kind from those given in the other gospels. John allows us a glimpse into the characters' lives—their relationships, their fears, their scars.

The Samaritan woman is like John's other character sketches in that he encourages us to engage her background using the facts he reports. But the apostle gives this dialogue a special place in his narrative. It is one of the longest unbroken conversations with an individual in his gospel, running about three hundred fifty words in the original (4:7–26). The complete story runs more than seven hundred words. The only other comparable dialogue is between Jesus and Nicodemus (3:1–21).[2]

John is saying, "Engage this woman attentively."

Even further, Jesus' teaching on divorce in other gospels exposes the woman's crucible.

In matters of divorce, Samaritans observed the Mosaic law in Deuteronomy 24:1–4. Montgomery notes that, in general, Samaritan legal documents were not admissible in Jewish courts, with the explicit exception of divorce papers.[3] This was an area (like others mentioned in chapter 3) in which there was interaction between the Jewish and Samaritan cultures, and in which there was some agreement about the form and content of those interactions.

Let's recall the law of divorce itself, both as Moses gave it and as Jesus interpreted it.

In Deuteronomy 24:1–4, Moses prescribes the reasons why a writ of divorce would be permitted and the limits of remarriage in such cases. The case he stipulates involves a man who discovers "some indecency" in his wife, *indecency* being a broad term describing any sexual exposure or perversion. The stipulations do not end there. Moses allows the husband to give her a writ of divorce, but goes on to consider what happens if she remarries, the second husband also discovers indecency, and also divorces her. Moses' ruling in this case is that the first husband may not take the woman back.

This law was a barrier to the serial abuse of women, but it was twisted into a justification for divorce.

In Matthew 19:1–9, the Pharisees ask Jesus about the lawfulness of a man divorcing his wife "for any reason at all." By this time, the permission to divorce a woman because of indecency had been generalized into permission to divorce because of anything that displeased the husband. When Jesus teaches that husband and wife are one flesh (quoting Genesis 2:24), the Pharisees counter by citing Deuteronomy 24. "Why then did Moses command to give her a certificate of divorce and send her away?"

Jesus' reply shows his view of the practice of divorce at this time: it was abusive toward women. "Because of your hardness of heart Moses permitted you to divorce your wives; but from the beginning it has not been this way." Jesus restores the law to its original purpose and teaches that remarriage after divorce for any other reason than the one stated by Moses, "immorality," is adultery.

We know a little more, then, about what the Samaritan woman had experienced in her divorces.

If Jesus thought Jewish divorces were abusive, it is hard to imagine him thinking any better of Samaritan ones. In all likelihood, the woman's first husband had slapped her with the label *indecent* as a legal justification for kicking her out merely because he didn't love her anymore. She had trusted this man, had displeased him somehow, and had been slandered as immoral with the complicity of a Samaritan priest. The woman could have been divorced numerous times in this manner without committing any immorality. She could have trusted another man, who wooed her in spite of her history, gave her promises of security, used her, and then treated her in the same way as her first husband.

This woman had probably been passed from man to man in a way that was systemically corrupt. She had seen what was underneath the white-robed piety of the Gerizim cult. So, if you wanted a penetrating critique of the corruption of Samaria, you would never learn as much from a Jewish Pharisee as you would from the woman at the well. In the crucible of her first marriages, she had learned truths about Samaritan religion from life—truths that really were true.

This point does not excuse her immorality. Jesus does not cancel out one person's sins by comparing them with another's, using the moral equivalence doctrine that lies at the heart of the accept-affirm approach. The woman's own testimony (John 4:29, 39) makes clear that he convicted her of sin, probably at more length than John records. "He told me all the things that I have done." No matter how unjust her first husband was, at some juncture she embraced immorality as a way of life.

But the point does clarify why Jesus brought up her past. He spoke to the whole context of her crucible within a false religion, the falsehood of which she did not need to hear explained. And Jesus spoke with discrimination, exposing the corruption of Samaritan men without excusing the woman's own sins.

This wise engagement was the soil in which the rest of the dialogue grew.

Truths Learned from a Contemporary Life

Sometimes the conclusions people draw from their crucibles are stunning.

George W. S. Trow, who died in December 2006, was an original and controversial media critic known for his withering attacks on the culture of television. His essay on media in the last half of the twentieth century, *My Pilgrim's Progress*, is structured around his memories of growing up in the 1950s.[4] The book yields page after page of insights into American life, written in an informal, almost gossipy style.

Consider one such insight. Trow fastens on the disappearance of "culture as something meant to protect," as a kind of shelter that preserves people against life's blows.

A typical definition of culture, he says, is now, "*My preferences, your preferences,* the sum total of whatever it is we happened to have liked. And if this year we like Debbie Reynolds and *Tammy and the Bachelor,* and last year we didn't, and the year before we liked Nine Inch Nails, and tomorrow we decide to take a look at the Butthole Surfers, well, that's just what we happen to want at the moment, and why shouldn't we?"[5] The significance of culture, he suggests, goes far beyond the superficialities of entertainment.

Culture should protect people when they fail. As individuals, we make plans for our lives that never come to completion, perhaps for a career, a lifestyle, or a relationship. "Our youthful ambitions are too unrealistic: 99.9 percent of us fail in the height of our ambition." When the cherished career, lifestyle, or relationship proves unattainable, a protective culture provides a place to land. "Let's call it a net. You fall from the high wire, and—golly, people have already predicted that possibly you would fall from the high wire, so fall into the net, and then you can regroup, make another, perhaps a better, decision or plan, and there you are."[6]

"Well, we don't have that." Trow says that authority figures do not even notice when people fail in their ambitions, much less predict it, and there is no net. So people crash:

> They pick themselves up, secretly, in the quiet of their own mind, having had to face some near infinite pain about delusion, and about lack of protection, about abandonment, about no one being there, about nothing being there; and they crawl away from their accident, and when at last they stand up again, if they do, they're a little deformed. And that's a lot of us now.[7]

So Trow identifies a reason for the extreme personal devastation around us. The networks of watchful people with authority have fallen apart. The people who might predict failure and act to preserve an individual no longer have foresight or resources.

I find this to be an arresting observation. It is another expression of the need for individuals to have strong identities and to live in strong communities. We've observed people's self-invented identities expressed through what they wear and carry around. We've analyzed how Starbucks treats people's fluid self-concept as the focus of its brand strategy. We've heard David Brooks explain the yearning of Bobos for old ways.

But Trow expresses this need not from the point of view of yearning, but of memory. *My Pilgrim's Progress* shows the disintegration of WASP culture among the very elite families that were supposed to pass it on—families such as Trow's own. It is a firsthand account of the slow-motion crucible that, Trow seems to say, left him "a little deformed."

He witnessed the dissolution of a culture of protection. There are truths about sin and righteousness that George Trow did not need to hear explained.

Another reason I find Trow's observation so significant is that evangelicals lack a story for him, a way to understand who he was and what he experienced. His world of the old WASP society in New York City dissolved into another one, the world of Diana Vreeland, Studio 54, James Taylor, and Sting—and not the media projections of those icons, but the individuals and settings themselves. The evangelical story for Trow's experience is not so much simplistic as nonexistent.

What other insightful people have evangelicals missed because they haven't cultivated the skills of engagement?

The Baptist at the Well

Suppose that our Baptist at Café Siddhartha talks with the woman, and that she sketches her memories of First Baptist of the Valley. We might imagine him lurching into the reject-correct approach. She shouldn't have abandoned Jesus just because her pastor was a fake. She shouldn't have wandered into Buddhism just because her parents split up. Of course, it's tragic that the people in her parents' church spent more time on creationism than on their walk with the Lord, but she shouldn't use their failure as a reason to seek spiritual wisdom from evolutionists.

But, again, we have to ask whether our Baptist has a larger reservoir of compassion than he might appear to have. He may be able to engage the woman deeply. If he has another story for this woman, if he has outgrown status insecurities, and if he understands her street philosophy, then he may earn the profound opportunity to hear the crucible she endured during her senior year of high school. He may hear a story that gives him respect for her insight. He may affirm that the crucible she endured was indeed tragic, that Christians often judge others such as evolutionists instead of examining themselves. Even more, if he knows the relational mode of dialogue (chapter 9) and Jesus' method of confrontation (chapter 10), he may give insights of his own that she will receive without hostility.

In that case—if he doesn't fit our story on the "typical evangelical"—then the very backwardness of his blue cardboard suit and his unnaturally black hair could be transformed into the signature of authenticity.

Here is a critical question. It presses the biblical mandate that evangelicals go further than cultural improvisations to reach the individuals of the diversity culture, and that they formulate a coherent worldview to enable wise engagement with others. Can we find a theology that will heal relationships at Café Siddhartha?

BECOMING A HEALER: CROSS THE BARRIER OF ENGAGEMENT

- Do an inventory of the non-Christian people in your life who are like George Trow—far from your racial, demographic, or cultural background. Rate how well you know each one. Are they intimate friends, familiar faces, or aliens from the next star system?
- Choose the one person whom you know best. Identify an

appropriate way to engage that person more deeply, a way that takes you one step further into the person's life. (For example, saying *hi* might be the next appropriate step. Or it might be a fifteen-minute coffee conversation.) Keep building this relationship to give yourself the opportunity to hear some of what he or she has experienced.

Part 2

FORMULATE THE MESSAGE

THE POWER OF SCRIPTURE

The *New York Times* story "Evangelicals Fear the Loss of Their Teenagers" was a balm to the souls at Café Siddhartha.[1]

Laurie Goodstein described a series of evangelical conferences organized by prominent leaders in 2006 to raise the alarm that large numbers of young people are leaving the faith. The meetings were prompted by the claim that "if current trends continue, only 4 percent of teenagers will be 'Bible-believing Christians' as adults. That would be a sharp decline compared with 35 percent of the current generation of baby boomers, and before that, 65 percent of the World War II generation."

Goodstein quoted Ron Luce, founder of the twenty-year-old ministry Teen Mania. "I'm looking at the data, and we've become post-Christian America, like post-Christian Europe. We've been working as hard as we know how to work—everyone in youth ministry is working hard—but we're losing."

Both youth pastors and evangelical youth themselves defined the problem in terms of peer pressure. They said that the culture of cynicism about God and sex, so dominant on MTV, the Internet, and every kind of pop music, is too powerful to oppose. Evangelical young people told Goodstein that "they felt like a tiny, beleaguered minority in their schools and neighborhoods."

When Goodstein gave a glimpse into youth pastors' strategy, one couldn't help but notice its shallowness.

Teen Mania has been organizing massive Christian rock festivals in sports stadiums around the country for the past fifteen years. Between October 2006 and May 2007, the group packed in forty shows, with seven hundred interns from Teen Mania's "Honor Academy" in Garden Valley, Texas, serving as roadies.

At the festivals, teenagers performed the ritual of writing down negative influences from brands, shows, and performers and then flooding the front of the stadium to throw the slips of paper into trash cans. Goodstein reported from a concert in Amherst, "Some teenagers threw away cigarette lighters, brand-name sweatshirts, Mardi Gras beads and CDs—one titled 'I'm a Hustla.'" Afterward, they bought T-shirts and CDs with the message, "Branded by God." Goodstein wrote, "Mr. Luce's strategy is to replace MTV's wares with those of an alternative Christian culture, so teenagers will link their identity to Christ and not to the latest flesh-baring pop star."

Luce referred to the two million teenagers who have attended Teen Mania's programs. He said, "That's more than Paul McCartney has pulled in."

For Goodstein, the quote was a guaranteed laugh line. In the context of evangelicals' unbroken failure to reach American youth, the claim encapsulated the yearning to be cool that churches so often call a "heart for the lost." *Times* readers were now assured that pastors who'd made their careers manipulating teenagers were going to fail.

Luce's efforts reflect a long-standing evangelical strategy: use the consumer society's techniques to advance the gospel. Speak to the fluid identities of consumers. Counter peer pressure from the world with a Christian brand. Massive concerts and rallies, an alternate universe of entertainment with a full complement of DVDs, T-shirts, and bumper stickers, offer Christians a hiding place in a secure demographic. Individuals don't have to think for themselves. They can swim in the correct groupthink instead.

Groupthink: The dynamic in which a group embodies right and wrong for all its members, suppressing questions in the name of loyalty.

Isolating the Conscience

The gospel of John displays a radically different approach. In John's narrative, just as in contemporary life, individuals stagger under the weight of cultural pressure to reject Jesus—pressure that John shows coming from political factions, from religious authorities, and from ethnic identities. But he shows another force that undermines this pressure, a challenge that is countercultural and that empowers individuals to think about God for themselves. It is the authority of Scripture.

The Old Testament is John's tool for isolating individual readers' consciences, a crowbar that pries individuals away from their groups by making God's standard of righteousness the sole measure of Jesus' truth. John starts prying in the prologue: "For the Law was given through Moses; grace and truth were realized through Jesus Christ" (1:17). Jesus and Moses are not in opposition to each other, as if Jesus replaced a law that was false or deficient. Rather, what Moses prescribed in the commandments came into being in the Word made flesh. John will show that Jesus is the completion of all righteousness, as defined by God's word, not by worldly loyalties.

Consider how the characters in John (2:13–22; 3:1–15; 5:18–47) have to choose between the Scriptures' teaching and their groups' demands.[2]

*   *   *

The odor of cattle and sheep hit John's nostrils when he entered the temple courtyard. The merchants had jammed the place with animals, anticipating the flood of Jews from around the world for Passover—all conveniently in need of sacrifices. There were so many beasts that the stench of their filth overwhelmed the more usual smell of blood from the altar.

John felt a poke in his ribs, but the place was so packed with men that he paid no attention. Another poke, harder this time. It was his brother James, who nodded toward Jesus, and then looked back at John with raised eyebrows. Jesus was tying ropes together with furious intensity—snapping his improvised whip a couple of times and then tying more ropes on. Jesus disappeared into the herds.

After the shouting started, John and the rest of the crowd were barely able to jump clear of the stampede. Among the sheep bleating and the oxen snorting, the hoofs ringing on the stone pavement, and the cries of the merchants and their customers, the noise was deafening. A flock of doves ripped from their cage, and disappeared over the temple. John heard the crash of a massive table against the pavement and saw temple coins rolling under the hoofs of panicked sheep. A little boy, no older than seven, stood against the wall screaming, the mud-tracks of his tears running down his cheeks, hands waving involuntarily and feet running in place, his eyes frantically searching the mayhem.

Jesus' voice rose above the din. "Stop making my Father's house a place of business!"

Finally the noise subsided, and the dust cleared to reveal the priests and scribes on the steps of the inner court, the brilliant colors of their robes glowing in the sun, their faces staring hard at Jesus and his disciples. John's adrenaline rush dissolved into nausea at the sight of them. He looked at James. "They will interrogate us! They already suspect Jesus, just like they suspected John the Baptist. How are we going to explain *this*? We don't have the education to argue with them. No one cares what fishermen say."

James stared at the rulers. Then he looked at John and shrugged. "It is written, 'Zeal for Your house will consume me.' David wasn't just talking about himself." He nodded again toward Jesus. "It fits him. We have to stand on that."

The rulers circled Jesus, demanding proof of his authority. When Jesus answered, "Destroy this temple, and in three days I will raise it up," the two brothers stood at his shoulders, along with Peter and the other disciples.

So when he was raised from the dead, His disciples remembered that he had said this; and they believed the Scripture and the word which Jesus had spoken.[3]

*   *   *

A lamp was about to go out, its wick smoldering.

Nicodemus fingered the fringes of his robe while he waved the smoke out of his eyes and tried to frame an answer to the young Galilean rabbi. Nicodemus had come in admiration and had delivered the council's finding. "We know that you have come from God as a teacher." Jesus had gained the approval of righteous men through his miracles and popularity, and the council's approval would make Jesus' way straight. Yet he treated Nicodemus as if age and position on the Sanhedrin were of no significance. What more did the Galilean want?

In the gloom, Nicodemus eyed Jesus, trying to discern what his face might tell, and reviewing the argument. "Unless one is born of water and the Spirit he cannot enter into the kingdom of God." "You must be born again." As if he, Nicodemus, and all the rulers were in the class of sinners! As if being sons of Abraham meant nothing! Was it nothing that they were heirs of the covenants? Was it of no account that God sent Moses and gave the law?

Finally Nicodemus sighed. "How can these things be?"

Jesus leaned forward, his face now revealed in a fading beam from the lamp. "Are you the teacher of Israel and do not understand these things?"

The conversation was deteriorating. What was Nicodemus supposed to report to the council? *The Galilean declares us sinners, even though we have the law.* Nicodemus could already hear his colleagues denouncing Jesus as no better than a Samaritan. He could already hear their questions about how he answered the turncoat.

Jesus reached over and extended the lamp's wick. "As Moses lifted up the serpent in the wilderness, even so must the Son of Man be lifted up; so that whoever believes will in Him have eternal life."

Moses and the plague of serpents! The sons of Abraham, the recipients of the law, the followers of Moses had to look upon the curse in order to live. This uneducated Galilean said he must become that curse to save the people. What rebuke was there for this? It stands written, just as Jesus said. But the council . . .

Nicodemus, who had first come to him by night, also came, bringing a mixture of myrrh and aloes, about a hundred pounds weight. So they took the body of Jesus and bound it in linen wrappings with the spices, as is the burial custom of the Jews.[4]

*   *   *

A Pharisee was standing with his two colleagues listening to the Galilean's defense against the charge of blasphemy. The Galilean had claimed that God was his father, and the crowd had grown as word spread that he was speaking. The Galilean said he was going to call witnesses. What witnesses could he possibly call to justify such a claim?

The Galilean looked directly at the Pharisee and the two others standing with him. "You have sent to John, and he has testified to the truth."

The Pharisee's gut tightened, but he gazed impassively at the upstart rabbi even as faces in the crowd turned to see whom the rabbi was addressing. *He remembers. He saw me in the delegation that questioned John the Baptist. And John did indeed say,* "Among you stands one whom you do not know. It is he who comes after me, the thong of whose sandal I am not worthy to untie." The Pharisee twisted one of his gold rings.

For another witness, the Galilean brought up the signs that he had done, which the council had already investigated and decided. The signs, they found, proved he came from God. That was why they had sent Nicodemus to meet him. *This one is clever. Very clever.* Twisting, twisting.

Now the Galilean was saying that the Father himself had testified about him in the Scriptures! "How can you believe, when you receive glory from one another and you do not seek the glory that is from the one and only God? Do not think that I will accuse you before the Father; the one who accuses you is Moses, in whom you have set your hope. For if you believed Moses, you would believe me, for he wrote about me. But if you will not believe his writings, how will you believe my words?"

He is as audacious as Nicodemus said. This is just like his argument from the plague of serpents: the bronze serpent referred to him. And what is the answer? The Pharisee kept twisting his ring and fought the instinct to look at his colleagues. He knew one glance would give him away as a doubter.

Nevertheless many even of the rulers believed in him, but because of the Pharisees they were not confessing him, for fear that they would be put out of the synagogue; for they loved the approval of men rather than the approval of God.[5]

*   *   *

Placing ourselves in the viewpoints of John's characters, as we've done above, we can see how John pits individuals against their groups. Whether the characters are Jesus' disciples or his enemies, the crowbar that pries them away from their worldly loyalty is their knowledge of Scripture. The pattern is consistent throughout John's gospel and ought to be considered one of his themes.

Confronting and Inviting the Reader

John makes two other uses of Scripture in his gospel.

First, he confronts the reader with historical facts by linking contemporaneous testimony to the prophecies of the Old Testament. The gospel of John compiles testimony from Moses, from John the Baptist, from Jesus, and from the apostle himself, and the narrative is crafted with the precision of a legal argument to prove that Jesus came from the Father to save sinners. This design empowers an individual to say, "My group has been ignoring history."

When John narrates the crucifixion of Jesus (19:17–37), for example, he is careful to quote prophecies showing the fulfillment of God's word. He explains the casting of lots for Jesus' tunic (19:23–25), Jesus' drinking of sour wine on a branch of hyssop (19:28–29), and the stabbing of Jesus with a spear (19:31–37) as being done to complete the descriptions of the crucifixion in the Old Testament. John is saying, "Here is what I saw, and it matches what God said."

In fact, when it comes to his ultimate goal in writing this gospel, John is famously blunt (20:30–31). His book joins the other sacred writings as a historical challenge to worldly loyalties, a challenge that all readers, at all times, from all groups will have to weigh for themselves. Jesus did many things that John does not record, "but these have been written so that you may believe that Jesus is the Christ, the Son of God; and that believing you may have life in His name." The care with which this testimony was crafted, and the boldness of its challenge, is evident in 21:24, where other disciples append their validation of John's record. "This is the disciple who is testifying to these things and wrote these things, and we know that his testimony is true."

Second, John's gospel invites the reader into deeper explorations of previous Scriptures. The narrative is rich with Old Testament allusions, weaving a literary tapestry of connections between Jesus and the prophets.

John's artistry is evident from his very first words (1:1–3). "In the beginning was the Word," John writes, alluding to the opening of Genesis. He repeats the allusion in verse 2, "He was in the beginning with God," and in verse 3 makes the point explicit: "All things came into being through Him, and apart from Him nothing came into being that has come into being." John does more than convey theological content; he almost insists that the reader reexamine Genesis 1 in light of what he has written.

There are more allusions in the first chapter. In verses 4–5, John brings in light and darkness, also from Genesis 1. In verse 14, the Word became flesh and *tabernacled*, or dwelt, among us, a reference to the revelatory and atoning functions of the tabernacle and the temple. Both allusions invite the reader to study, meditate on, and apply more truth about Jesus from the Old Testament.

The fourth gospel is dense with such invitations.

John's narrative, then, unveils an approach to evangelism that may be shocking to evangelicals. Instead of countering group pressure by trying to build up a new mass identity, John frees the individual conscience to make decisions on its own by supplying alternative information. Scripture undermines the authority of the groups that stand between individuals and God and opens a direct line to God himself.

Scripture and the Samaritan Woman

The strategy of undermining human authority with Scripture is a key part of Jesus' approach to the Samaritan woman.

Late in the conversation, she seems only to bring up a point of ritual correctness (4:19–20). "Sir, I perceive that You are a prophet. Our fathers worshiped in this mountain, and you people say that in Jerusalem is the place where men ought to worship." She is certainly raising the issue of the right location for worshiping God—perhaps the most distinctive claim Samaritans made upon each other's loyalty. But behind her statement is a question about the authority supporting that claim—Samaritan texts.

The Samaritans had their own copies of the Pentateuch, an entire textual tradition whose origins provoke scholarly debate to this day. Ancient sources as diverse as the Talmud and the Patristic writers assumed the existence of and sometimes even used the Samaritan Pentateuch. The texts were lost to European scholarship until the Renaissance humanist Pietro della Valle bought a copy at Damascus in 1616.[6] Scholars say that the Samaritan Pentateuch shows remarkable similarity to the Masoretic text, the authoritative Hebrew manuscripts, in spite of having developed independently.[7]

But on the issue of where to worship Yahweh, the Samaritans made important changes. Mt. Gerizim is substituted for Mt. Ebal "as the place where the law was to be written on the stones of the altar (Deut. 27:4)."[8] There were frequent glosses in Samaritan texts, such as the claim written in the margin of one copy around Deuteronomy 5:6 by an anonymous scribe claiming to be a descendant of Aaron and seeking to legitimize worship on Gerizim: "I Abishua, son of Phineas, son of Eleazar, son of Aaron—may YHWH's favor and glory be theirs—wrote the holy book in the gate of the tabernacle on Mount Gerizim in the 13th year after that [sic] the Israelites ruled the land of Canaan in its borders round about. I make known YHWH." James Montgomery, after quoting the gloss, calls it "preposterous."[9]

The Samaritans used their version of the Pentateuch as a justification for worshiping on their mountain rather than going to Jerusalem. When the woman at the well confronts Jesus with Mt. Gerizim, then, she is not just talking about cultic practices, but about the authority of the texts on which those practices were based.

Jesus first addresses the immediate issue of location, a reply we'll consider more thoroughly in chapters 6 and 10. He says that neither Mt. Gerizim nor Jerusalem will be relevant to the worship of the Father (4:21). This removes a key barrier between the two as individuals from hostile cultures.

But in the rest of Jesus' reply, he focuses on the issue behind the Mt. Gerizim controversy—the texts that validate Samaritan worship.

"You worship what you do not know," he tells her (4:22). The second-person verbs *worship* and *know* are plural, referring to the Samaritan community. Jesus asserts that the Samaritans have the right object of worship, the Lord, but that they worship him in ignorance. He is referring to their version of the Pentateuch, and to their limitation of God's word to the Mosaic law alone. The Samaritans could never follow the prophets who came later, all of whom focus on the Jerusalem temple as the center of the kingdom. The Samaritans were therefore ignorant of God's plan for salvation from sin and for future human history. For instance, they never developed a full doctrine of Messiah. Montgomery writes,

> A prophet after the manner of Moses (Dt. 18) was what the Samaritans desired in their Messiah; this notion accordingly limited the Samaritan ideas. He was to be a Revealer of hidden or lost truths like the one the Samaritan woman had in mind, and inasmuch as there could be no greater prophet than Moses nor one equal to him, the Messiah is an entirely inferior personage.[10]

Jesus makes the contrast between Samaritans and Jews explicit. "We worship what we know, for salvation is from the Jews." Israel had the detailed revelation of God's plan of redemption and a fully developed doctrine of the coming Messiah, so they could worship the Father with an understanding of their place in that plan.

Jesus presses the matter of the full Old Testament further (4:23). "But an hour is coming, and now is, when the true worshipers will worship the Father in spirit and truth." While there will not be a physical location for worship, there will be another kind of zone for it. The Father requires worship in the "spirit and truth" zone. That is, a true worshiper has both the inward reality of the new birth (spirit)[11] and the objective reality of scriptural teaching (truth). Since the Samaritans have no source for understanding the new birth and lack the full canon, the woman will have to choose between her community and her God.

Jesus challenges the woman at the well with the authority of Scripture. He isolates her conscience from the authority of her group and teaches her to think for herself about who the Father is and what he requires.

Scripture Versus Groupthink Today

Many evangelicals are suspicious of the slogan "Think for yourself."

It's associated with relativism and suspicion of authority, the loosening of moral standards, and the growth of alternative lifestyles. People who think for themselves get into trouble.

The slogan is loaded with personal baggage. Generations of evangelical parents have seen it thrown at their children and feel it has undermined their children's love and loyalty. The philosophy of doing "what's right for you" is not abstract to most older evangelicals, but is a toxin that poisoned their families, a toxin against which they had no antidote. To them, "Think for yourself" means "I'm not listening anymore." It provokes anger and even helplessness.

Evangelicals, in other words, have been assaulted by ideologies that dissolve bonds of loyalty and that have plunged the entire Western world into social upheaval. The autonomy of the individual has been intensified by media that make information ever more accessible—formerly television, now the Internet. The individual's liberty has been sung in rock and roll and praised in film. Words such as *loyalty* can hardly be uttered anymore without irony or defensiveness. This has been an especially bitter season for those of the World War II generation, who experienced solidarity in desperate trials and who knew the power of sticking together.

To most evangelicals, the diversity culture, with its "think for yourself" philosophy, appears to be anarchy. But I believe this appearance is deceptive. What we actually face is the tyranny of mass opinion.

In a consumer society of soft identities, one that requires people to invent themselves, individuals cannot think freely, but are obligated to follow the stampedes of their various demographics. If persons are defined by what they consume—their T-shirts, their tunes, their toys—then the only measure of their viability is the consumption of others around them. As we have seen, the authority of Starbucks is obeyed and just as often resented because it reassures its core customers about who they are. The consumer society is driven by a very needy self—an other-directed self.

So the dynamic of people adhering closely to the groups they think are safe, the opinions they know are approved, and the lifestyles they see as well-fortified—the dynamic of loyalty, even on the shallow foundation of consumerism—is far from dead.

Indeed, in some ways, the new loyalty to one's demographic is harder to break than the old loyalty to God, family, and community. The cultural revolutions of the twentieth century enticed people to ignore restrictions that were ancient. But demographic loyalties are powered by the voltage of Now. Former loyalties could be broken because their enforcers were few—easily confused, inarticulate in the new ways, easily deceived. But the mass culture of the consumer society has the power of a mob—it has watchers everywhere, it thrives on the clarity of slogans, and it punishes nonconformity, making Christian young people feel like "a tiny, beleaguered minority in their schools and neighborhoods." The old loyalties could be broken because they were inflexible. The new are constantly changing.

The grip of demographic loyalties is truly a tyranny, and it cannot be broken by creating counter-demographics as shelters. The strategy of massive rock concerts and stadium meetings, the naive evangelical faith in numbers and the power of mass media, and the pathetic yearning to bring in more kids than Paul McCartney all reflect the superficiality of evangelical thinking about the times we're living in. We cannot break the power of groupthink by opposing it with more groupthink.

We need to restore one of our oldest appeals: *Sola scriptura*.

The signature of biblical Christianity has always been freedom of thought. John's gospel was more than a millennium ahead of its time in the boldness of its appeal to the individual's own conscience. Free thought is an evangelical heritage from the Reformation, now stolen by those who promise freedom and deliver conformity. Free thought has always been enabled by the Scriptures, which give to any person the power to know God and hear from him directly, apart from the mediation of any institution or group.

> *Sola Scriptura*: "Scripture alone," the Reformation doctrine that every human authority is subordinate to the Bible.

The evangelical strategy of creating a godly brand identity has two profound faults.

First, it discards the very theology of conversion. Individuals do not come to know Christ because they join a flood of people rushing to the front of a stadium to burn their hip-hop CDs. The mass psychology of man does not produce the righteousness of God. Individuals come to know Christ because their consciences are isolated from the standards and worldview they have always assumed—even if they grew up in church—and are made accountable directly to God. The force that accomplishes this is God's Word. Once an individual is thinking for himself, he is ready to meet Jesus.

Second, the evangelical brand strategy is more than a theological crime;

it is a cultural blunder. The diversity culture hates the consumerism it cannot quite leave behind. The shallow TV culture became a joke long ago. The language and strategies of marketing are suspect among the young. One of the most potent appeals of the Internet is that it empowers an individual to investigate on her own, to form networks around her obscure interests, to construct her life off the standard tracks.

Church growth technicians, with predictable timing, became skilled at applying demographics to their strategies just when the very analysis of segmentation became too generalized to reflect people's actual behavior. The reason why teenagers leave evangelical churches is no mystery: they can see that churches have abandoned the power of God and embraced the waning power of pop.

The first thing the Baptist at Café Siddhartha needs to articulate to the woman he meets is, "You can know the truth for yourself, and the truth will set you free."

BECOMING A HEALER: ESCAPE YOUR GROUPTHINK

- Identify the most powerful group in your life. Which group has the most sway over your important life decisions: family, peers, colleagues, those who attend your church?
- What kinds of pressure from this group are most effective in swaying your decisions?
- Do you find yourself using pressure on others in your group to sway their decisions?
- Identify one area in which you believe the Bible calls you to do something contrary to your group's ways. Specifically, where do you find that call in the Bible? What are you going to do about it?

6

THE POWER OF COMMUNITY

In my grandmother's kitchen hangs a carved wooden spoon. The Danish custom was for a man to carve such a spoon with his own design, and give it to the woman he wanted to marry. Consider the power of this vanished ritual.

The carved spoon was a simple, clear message. The moment a man held it before a woman's eyes, she knew his soul. When she took the spoon, the two were initiated into a new status in their community. The gift was so simple that it combined the broadest public announcement—something a small child would understand as well as the oldest widow—with the most intimate private whispers. It was also a demonstration of devotion, evidence of patient labor and purposeful tenderness.

Such a token would be unique, irreplaceable. Even if two men's designs were similar, the impact of their hands would be like the call of a voice. The ridges left by a man's knife, the roughness or smoothness, the complexity of the ornaments, would all be as individual as handwriting. No two women would receive the same gift, any more than they would marry the same man.

Today a man who carved such a piece of folk art to propose marriage would be called eccentric at best. A woman who accepted him would be called special. The ritual has no meaning because the culture that used to perform it has disintegrated.

To express ourselves in a consumer society, we no longer make things. We buy things.

I have a theory that many people want to be in a movie. In the absence of genuine individuality, they envision themselves in cinematic clichés—the swelling orchestra and flattering camera angles. Patricia Cohen's *New York Times* piece, "Love, Honor, Cherish and Buy," gives the reader a tour of a bridal exposition, where brides-to-be can learn how to create their perfect day.[1]

The average budget for this film is $27,000—an average, Cohen says, "the industry likes to cite."

That figure gets you the videographer without whom it wouldn't be cinema. It pays for set-design elements such as "a 4½ foot tower of calla lilies ($700)" and the limo, which on wedding special is $720 for three and a half hours and includes "an aisle runner, Champagne, bar and 'horns' that play a recording of 'Here Comes the Bride' when the car stops."

The budget buys perks for the cast, such as "a drugstore-style photo booth" at $1,595 for four hours. You can have it and an attendant for five hours for a mere $100 more. You can rent "a portable toilet with oak cabinetry, marbled sinks, Oriental rugs and a black-tie attendant ($3,495 for eight hours)." There are half-liter bottles of water with labels bearing pictures of the bride and groom at $48 a case.

The budget includes the band you're "bringing up from New Orleans," because every movie needs a soundtrack.

And don't forget the stars.

For him, "a long, white buttonless tuxedo with a mandarin collar ($119 to rent)." For her, wedding specials on teeth whitening, laser cellulite reduction and hair removal, and weight-loss.

For both, insurance to protect the perfect day. From WedSafe, a policy of $25,000 for $295 "protects against bad weather, death or an illness that forces cancellation."

Knowing that people want to be in a movie, "the industry" uses the hardsell. Fill out a card at the expo and you'll be mailed, e-mailed, and called by dozens of vendors. The videographer tells you that if you don't hire him "your happiness will be lost, your memories will be lost." Best not even to announce you're shopping for a wedding because "vendors know that 'if it's a wedding, you're going to spend more.'"

But hiding the fact that you're getting married may not be wise either.

Suppose you don't want the limo wedding special for $720 for three and a half hours of driving, Champagne, and tuneful "horns." Suppose you just want a normal limo for four hours at $576. Saleswoman: "You can't. If the bride and groom are in the car, you can't do it. We've pulled in, and there is a woman in a wedding dress, and they can't do it. The car had to leave."

Such is the degradation of our culture that rituals come in customizable packages from an industry. In place of simple directness, we have ostentation. In place of unique expressions of love and devotion, we have sentimentality. In place of the crude truth of life with another human being, we have the perfect cinematic lie.

We have lost a sense of belonging, and the people of the diversity culture know it.

> **Belonging**: An irrevocable connection that binds two or more unique individuals.

The New Family

One of the themes running through the gospel of John is that the Father and the Son are creating a new family of human beings. It is a theme that should speak to the needs of modernity's emotional refugees. But in places, John's narrative expresses Christ's embrace of his family in terms that are shockingly physical. There's something unsettling about John's reclining on Jesus' bosom.

The theme tightens its grip on us in John's prologue before we're aware of its significance. Jesus is the Creator, the source of all life. "All things came into being through Him, and apart from Him nothing came into being that has come into being" (1:3). So when he came into the world, he came "to His own," the possessions he had made and invested with life. But they did not "receive" him (1:10–11). He was not greeted, not acknowledged, not loved. The essence of human "darkness" is our refusal to greet our Creator with an acknowledgment of belonging.

The redemptive mission of Christ is to create a new intimacy between human beings and the Father. "But as many as received Him, to them He gave the right to become children of God . . ." (1:12). Jesus gives a birth from above—a new life, a new kind of belonging. The right to become children of God is given to those "who believe in His name," who receive Jesus and are "born of God."

The intimacy of this new family is concentrated without sentimentality into the words *children* and *born*. God has a bond with those who receive Jesus, a bond as unthinking and primal as the one I have with my two boys. I gave them life. I held them while they were still slathered in their mother's blood. Mine was the first look at their faces, and even as their faces become square and hard, I know every contour. I know their voices, the wit in their eyes, the push and pull of their limbs, the peculiar waywardness of their hair. No man will know them with the depth of my knowledge. They are mine—irrevocably mine. And I am theirs.

This is the kind of belonging that John's prologue summons to our senses.

Fatherhood, in John's gospel, determines whether individuals belong to darkness or light, as Jesus teaches Nicodemus. "Truly, truly, I say to you, unless one is born again he cannot see the kingdom of God" (3:3).

Earthly fatherhood is of no significance to Christ (8:37–44). To Jews, Jesus says, "I know that you are Abraham's descendants; yet you seek to kill Me, because My word has no place in you" (v. 37). Abraham's physical paternity lacks the power to give righteousness to their hearts. Their spiritual father has already endowed them with wickedness. "I speak the things which I have seen with My Father; therefore you also do the things which you heard from your father" (v. 38). The spiritual legacy of Abraham does not belong to them, and God is not their father. "If God were your Father, you would love Me, for I proceeded forth and have come from God" (v. 42).

Their father is, in fact, the devil.[2] "He was a murderer from the beginning, and does not stand in the truth because there is no truth in him. Whenever he speaks a lie, he speaks from his own nature, for he is a liar and the father of lies" (v. 44). The intimate, primal belonging that they should enjoy with their Creator, they have instead with Satan.

Jesus compares the power of belonging in God's new family to a fold of sheep (10:14–16). "I am the good shepherd, and I know My own and My own know Me." What kind of knowledge is this? It is the same as the intimacy between the Father and the Son. Jesus knows the sheep "even as the Father knows Me and I know the Father" (v. 15a). What level of commitment is there on the shepherd's part? His commitment is total and unhesitating: "I lay down My life for the sheep" (v. 15b).

This comparison between God's new family and a fold of sheep yields another fact. Jesus has sheep outside of Israel. "I must bring them also, and they will hear My voice; and they will become one flock with one shepherd" (v. 16). God's new family is characterized both by wide diversity and by powerful union through the voice of Christ.

Jesus makes an explicit connection between his atoning death and the new family bond. He refers to his washing of the disciples' feet, symbolic of his atonement (13:1–5), and gives a new commandment, "that you love one another, even as I have loved you, that you also love one another" (13:34). The same totality of commitment that the shepherd shows for the sheep, the sheep are to show for the other sheep. God's new family exhibits an observable and profound love. In fact love is to be the most powerful identifying mark of this family. "By this all men will know that you are My disciples, if you have love for one another" (v. 35).

Jesus goes even further and describes the origin of this love (17:20–24). Praying to his Father, Jesus makes his deepest desires known for the church, those in the future who will believe. He desires "that they may all be one; even as You, Father, are in Me and I in You, that they also may be in Us, so that the world may believe that You sent Me" (v. 21). The unity of the new family is an extension of the unity between Jesus and the Father. It is also an extension of the Father's glory. "The glory which You have given Me I have given to them, that they may be one, just as We are one" (v. 22). The essence of this unity is "I in them and You in Me" (v. 23).

The new family's bond is beyond primal—a direct connection back to the source of all life.

The family becomes reality in John's gospel after Jesus' resurrection (20:17). Jesus tells an ecstatic Mary Magdalene to stop clinging to him, "but go to My brethren." This is the first and only time in John that Jesus refers to his disciples as his family. Jesus is emphatic about what the word *brethren* means to him. He sends the message, "I ascend to My Father and your Father, and My God and your God." Mary is the first Christian to testify that Jesus' death and resurrection have created a new family of human beings.

This new family is the source of belonging that ought to be attracting individuals away from Café Siddhartha.

The Samaritan Woman's New Family

Jesus' dialogue with the Samaritan woman is a significant development of John's theme. As we have seen, the woman is like many people in America's diversity culture. She has a soft identity, and a painful history with her own group. Jesus has spoken directly to both of these issues, further weakening her identity as a Samaritan and confronting her many marriages. When Jesus is finished guiding her through her past, she therefore raises the most pertinent issue. *If I'm a sinner and my heritage cannot give me spiritual life, with whom do I worship?*

We can easily miss the significance of what she asks. She knows nothing of megachurches that present spirituality as a consumer item. She knows nothing of the arts of self-presentation by which we mark our identities—she doesn't have a Gerizim T-shirt. There is, for this woman, no such thing as conversion in the sense we know it today, the sense of a rootless and autonomous consumer renaming herself and attaching to a new group.

In order to convert, the woman has to disentangle herself from the intricate claims of her culture. She and Jesus share a perspective of ethnic rituals, of roots, of hand-carved tokens. Conversion for her means departure from her people, from every narrative that tells her who she is. So when she brings up the issue of whether an individual should worship at Gerizim or Jerusalem, she is asking whether there is any community to which she can belong (4:19–20). The autonomous life doesn't exist. So, what city does the well of living water nourish? Can the prophet point to it?

He can. "Woman, believe Me, an hour is coming when neither in this mountain nor in Jerusalem will you worship the Father" (4:21). If she has been convicted of sin—and she has (4:29)—if she needs to offer sacrifice, and if she is uncertain of where to do so, then this statement from the rabbi is a powerful source of hope. There *is* another community.

Her hope has another focus in his statement. Jesus refers not to "God," as he did earlier (4:10), but to *the Father*. He is saying that she, an abused and cynical sinner, unloved and suspicious, has a family. God is not to be worshiped generically, but as the very giver of her life, as the one who knows her, who watches over her, as the one who looks at her and says, "Mine." This other community is not just open to her, but is the family to which she *belongs*.

So, hearing that the Jewish and Samaritan communities are irrelevant now, she would long to know where the new family worships. Jesus teaches her that the family worships not in a physical location, but in a spiritual zone (4:23–24). "But an hour is coming, and now is, when the true worshipers will worship the Father in spirit and truth" (v. 23).

The new birth—being born of God (1:13), baptized with the Holy Spirit (1:33), being born in the Spirit (3:5)—is the first part of the zone in which a child in the new family worships. She worships "in spirit."[3] Jesus has already promised her that, if she asks him, he will give her "living water" that will become "a well of water springing up to eternal life" (4:10, 14).

Truth is the second part of this zone. Jesus, as we have seen, specifically refers to scriptural truth, the revelation of God's redemptive plan given to and through the Jewish people (4:22). Jesus is teaching her that the truth that "we [the Jews] know" is not restricted in its application to one ethnicity, but applies to all peoples in the world, including Samaritans.

This new family of true worshipers is so treasured by the Father that "such people the Father seeks to be His worshipers" (4:23). He seeks them because they will be born into his very nature. "God is spirit, and those who worship Him must worship in spirit and truth" (4:24).

Jesus does not merely promise the woman salvation from sin as an individual, but promises her a place to belong. It is the power of this promise that evangelicals should exhibit to the diversity culture.

The New Family Today

In his gospel, John teaches that there is a second divinely appointed means of evangelism. Preaching the Scriptures to free consciences from the tyranny of the world's darkness is not enough. The exhibition of love by the church in its many gatherings is just as significant a part of the light of Christ.

In one sense, this is hardly news. Every Christian agrees. We yearn for our churches to exhibit the love of Christ more. But so often this reduces to a wish that fellow believers would be nicer—especially to us. There is an empty sentimentality in much of our love-talk.

What John shows us is radical. From an ancient context in which *belonging* was a tangible fact of ethnicity, city, language, class, training, family, and father, John preaches that we belong to our Creator. We belonged to him from the beginning. Because the Son has "brought the Father out"—a literal rendering of John 1:18, meaning that Jesus has made the Father visible in human flesh—we belong to him anew by faith. And because the Son gave his life for us, we belong not only to him but to each other.

When you become a Christian, a bond fastens to your soul that endows you with a new story and a new identity. It's a bond of love, to be sure, but a bond nevertheless.

The contrast with the culture of evangelicalism could not be more stark. I am not thinking of the Christian media, of evangelical preaching, or even of its marketing strategies. When I refer to culture, I am thinking of the daily rhythms of local churches.

Churches are now segmented, structured according to demographic distinctives that speak to people's shallowest identities. The reader can identify which church in town is the hot place for young married couples to go, which church has nailed youth ministry, which is doing the emergent café thing, and which is full of the elderly. Music is the most obvious appeal to demographic segments. But there are other appeals too: the location and design of the facility, the pastor's haircut, even the arrangement of the chairs. Megachurches succeed in holding large numbers of people because they offer a wide variety of demographic storefronts with which people can identify.

Whatever the typical megachurch is, however you evaluate it, it does not offer John's kind of belonging. Rather, it offers the autonomy you get from your homepage. You choose the inputs. You never have to see anything you don't want to see. You do not have to reveal more about yourself than you want. In the rhythms of daily life, the body of Christ has become a customizable package offered by an industry. I believe this quality is a major reason why megachurches have failed to penetrate the diversity culture. They are not meeting its most powerful felt need.

The superficiality of the megachurch is easy to attack. Nothing is simpler now than reducing the megachurch pastor to the caricature of an ambitious, craven manipulator. But I see two problems with this kind of rhetoric.

> **Autonomy**: An independence so extreme that you become a law to yourself.

First of all, for talented, ambitious visionaries, building a megachurch has got to be one of the least rewarding paths to notoriety. The stress of ministry at this scale has ground more than one man to powder—everything from budget shortfalls to staff rivalries to factionalism in the pews. And for what? Megachurch pastors are targets of controversy both inside their churches and outside. Very few of them attain wealth, but live far below the lifestyle of their corporate peers.

Pastors build these churches, on the whole, because they have given their lives for the kingdom of Christ.

Secondly, I think many evangelicals may prefer demographic identification, with its fluidity, to the genuine belonging described by John. They may like their storefront within the embrace of the spiritual mall. They may like disappearing into the crowd, the comfort of never having their image challenged by association with the uncool, of never having to endure the tension of a status clash. Church, after all, is their haven.

So I don't think the superficiality of today's megachurch is the result of a few superslick pastors. I think it may be a direct expression of the will of the people. You can argue that their pastors should challenge them more, lead more courageously, sacrifice growth to integrity. But the reality is that the growth of megachurches is the result of many evangelicals making the same choices, adopting a religious lifestyle that matches American consumerism. The responsibility for megachurch superficiality is broadly shared.

I think evangelicals face stark options. Belong to each other in community or die. The gospel was not designed to be exhibited by people who all dress and talk the same, and who are all the same age. I believe the evangelical failure to convert the diversity culture is a result of evangelicals' having strategized their way beyond love.

You can break this suffocating superficiality in your church by undermining its daily rhythms. You can act on any of three principles:

1. *You belong to those who are older and younger.* Jesus has made you part of the same household as those of other generations. You can look for opportunities to make that bond of kinship a fact of daily life rather than a nice idea. Start by invading an age-defined program at church where you don't fit, either by volunteering to help with those who are younger or by attending the events of those who are older. Become as much a part of their lives as they will permit. You can see your peers some other time. Church is for growing beyond your current horizons.

2. *You belong to those who have different lifestyles.* Jesus has made you part of the same household as those who have different tastes and economic priorities. The size of their families may be the opposite of yours. Their music

may be impossible for you to enjoy. The cars they drive, the condition in which they keep their cars, the clothes they wear, the hairstyles they get, the amount and quality of makeup they use, the age and location of their homes—all the things they fill their lives with may tell you that you don't belong to them. But you do. Find an area of service in your church where there is the highest concentration of diverse lifestyles, and serve there. Interact with them and discover what it is that Christ sees in them. Get as far into their lives as they will permit.

3. *You belong to those from another educational background.* Jesus has made you part of the same household as those who received training that you may find alien and threatening. They may have been trained to focus on problems that you don't care about, going into far greater detail about those problems than you can stand. They may not have been trained to deal with any of the problems you do care about. They may approach work from an alternate universe. They may handle negotiation and decision-making in ways that you find narrow, contentious, and obsessive. Their training may tell you that you don't belong to them. But you do. So don't work exclusively with the people who were educated as you were. Find people whose training threatens you, work on a project with them, and grow in love.

The individual who acts on any of these principles will get caught up in a new way of life. He will use the rhythms of the daily schedule to learn how to love. She will value the individuality of other Christians more, will develop a unique role in a little platoon, will find larger significance in the corporate decisions of the church, will see the power of prayer and discipleship. The individual will have a community, and will be able to say to patrons at Café Siddhartha, "Look at this community. This is what Christ does."

But in order to act on any of the three principles, the individual will need to stop looking for the church that meets his needs. The individual will need to confront her own consumerism. In order to see the power of community, the individual will have to embrace belonging.

BECOMING A HEALER: EMBRACE YOUR COMMUNITY

- Identify the parts of your life that you most want to control—for example your schedule, music, or diet.
- What are you saying about yourself in each of these parts of your life? To what extent do they form your "invented self" (see chapter 2)?
- Choose one of these parts to yield for the sake of joining other Christians.

7

THE POWER OF TESTIMONY

On January 15, 2007, the *New York Times* ran a piece by Louise Story, "Anywhere the Eye Can See, It's Likely to See an Ad."[1] Her piece made the most e-mailed list for a day. Interest in the article may have reflected how many *Times* readers are in public relations, or it may have expressed the irritability of a public besieged by salespeople. The article portrayed the minute level to which marketing has to descend in order to get messages to consumers. Think eggs.

I believe that inside many evangelical pastors is a marketing executive yearning to be free. Pastors have to dream up ways to lure people into the Bible, and they become skilled at doing so—or they don't survive.

So there has long been an obsession among evangelicals with advertising. The "I Found It!" campaign in the 1970s was the first evangelical attempt I can remember to use mainstream marketing to spread the gospel: there were billboards with people smiling at you, there were buttons with the slogan on it, there were posters, all printed on a solid blue background. Everything begged you to ask, "Whadja find?"

My recollection is that the campaign blew through our church and had no discernible impact.

According to Story, impact is getting harder to achieve. "Yankelovich, a market research firm, estimates that a person living in a city 30 years ago saw up to 2,000 ad messages a day, compared with up to 5,000 today." I don't even want to know the per-minute number. The firm surveyed

4,110 people about marketing, half of whom thought it was "out of control." Money is a good measure of how out of control it has become. In 2000, advertisers spent $24 million on something called "alternative media." Last year the figure was $387 million.

What is all this money paying for?

Messages on subway turnstiles, Chinese food cartons, motion sickness bags, airport security trays, the paper liners of examination tables in doctors' offices, and tray tables on planes. Also radio ads on school buses, aroma-emitting displays at bus stops, digital screens that replace old fashioned billboards, projections onto buildings and sidewalks, interactive floor displays, product placement in TV shows and movies, video screens in taxicabs, shirt boxes and hanging bags from dry cleaners, and . . . stamped supermarket eggs.

Story quoted one ad executive. "We never know where the consumer is going to be at any point in time, so we have to be everywhere. Ubiquity is the new exclusivity."

The problem is that the average person sees advertising as annoying, invasive, and disrespectful. Overt marketing is no longer a credible source of information.

But somewhere, some pastor read this article and thought, "We should be as smart as the marketing people. We should make the gospel ubiquitous. We could put *I Found It!* on airline tray tables, project it on buildings around town, print it on blue examination table liners. We could stamp it on eggs!"

Two ironies are inescapable.

Evangelicals have a knack for riding waves that broke years before. It was decades ago that advertising lost its mystique and became a joke, and now marketing directors struggle to stay fresh. Yet churches are watchful for the next advertising bonanza, like *The Passion of the Christ*, as if it's the Spirit descending like a dove.

But more painful is the reality that followers of Christ should already have that quality advertisers pay $387 million per year to attain: ubiquity.

How does it happen that evangelicals are in every neighborhood, profession, and social stratum, yet the message of their lives dissolves into the culture?

The Persuasive Presence

John's gospel has another theme we need to examine. The strategy of undermining worldly loyalties with the Scriptures and of displaying love in community involves a third component that closes the deal—or rather, not a component but a person. This person takes the Scriptures and the love of God's new family and applies them directly to the souls of individuals. The ultimate persuader is Jesus himself.

In his prologue (1:14–18), John teaches the essence of Jesus' mission. Since "no one has seen God at any time," Jesus came into the world to "explain" the Father, or translated

> **Persuasion**: The art of moving a person from one resolution to a new one.

literally, to "bring him out." The separation between the Father and the world had to be bridged. So, "the Word became flesh and dwelt among us," displaying the Father's glory as his "only begotten." For the apostle John, human darkness is so impenetrable that no argument will persuade people to believe. The Scriptures can loosen their loyalties with new information. The new family can lure them with love. But only the display of grace and truth in Jesus himself will finally persuade.

For instance, when John the Baptist teaches the significance of his baptism with water, he points directly to Jesus (1:29–34). Jesus is the one who "baptizes in the Holy Spirit." As a witness of Jesus' water baptism, John says, "I myself have seen, and have testified that this is the Son of God." Later, when John is confronted with his loss of followers to Jesus, he replies that the trend is good (3:27–30). True spiritual life can only come from the Son, because "a man can receive nothing unless it has been given him from heaven." John told everyone from the start of his ministry, "I am not the Christ." John is merely a friend of the bridegroom who rejoices at the bridegroom's call. "He must increase, but I must decrease."

Jesus makes the same assertions about himself in breathtaking ways. He offers no signs of his authority to the Jews who demand them except his own presence.

When, for instance, Jews want a sign like the manna in the wilderness, Jesus replies that "the bread of God is that which comes down out of heaven, and gives life to the world." They respond, "Lord, always give us this bread." Jesus says, "I am the bread of life; he who comes to Me will not hunger, and he who believes in Me will never thirst" (6:30–35). The sign that persuades is Jesus himself.

In another confrontation (10:24–30), the Jews say, "How long will You keep us in suspense? If You are the Christ, tell us plainly." Jesus refuses to deal with them on these terms. He did tell them his identity, but they did not believe. He explains, "My sheep hear My voice, and I know them, and they follow Me; and I give eternal life to them, and they will never perish; and no one will snatch them out of My hand." All the sheep need to follow the shepherd is his voice.

Even when Jesus ministers to a dear friend in a moment of grief, he makes his own presence the focus of attention (11:23–27). His friend Martha is able to articulate the right doctrine to Jesus about the resurrection of her brother Lazarus at the last day. But Jesus knows that she doubts his personal faithfulness because he did not come to heal Lazarus in time. So he says to Martha, "I am the resurrection and the life; he who believes in Me will live even if he dies, and everyone who lives and believes in Me will never die." He sharpens the impact by asking his grieving friend, "Do you believe this?" Martha confesses that Jesus is "the Son of God, even He who comes into the world." Jesus will not even argue for his personal fidelity. He will only assert his presence.

We can see why Jesus maintains this focus while he walks the earth. But Jesus does not change focus when he prepares the disciples for his physical absence. After he is raised from the dead and ascends into heaven, his direct spiritual presence will be more important than ever.

The presence of Jesus will be the key to the disciples' fruitfulness. "Abide in Me, and I in you" (15:4). The disciples, he teaches, are like branches growing from a vine: they cannot bear fruit unless they maintain their connection. Abiding in Jesus means drawing nourishment and energy from him personally, as a constant and natural source of life. "I am the vine, you are the branches; he who abides in Me and I in him, he bears much fruit, for apart from Me you can do nothing" (15:5).

The presence of Jesus through the Holy Spirit will also persuade the world of its darkness (16:7–15). The Spirit's coming is to the disciples' advantage, because he will "convict the world concerning sin and righteousness and judgment." The Spirit "will not speak on His own initiative." He only delivers what he hears from Jesus himself. "He will glorify Me, for He will take of Mine and will disclose it to you." It is, in other words, for the impact of his own persuasive powers that Jesus sends the Spirit.

The disciples are not to worry about the world's hatred (15:18–25), the persecutions from the Jewish leaders (16:1–4), or Jesus' own death (16:16–22). Even though all these things will drive them into deep discouragement, the world's most opaque darkness is powerless to overcome the light of Jesus' presence (1:5).

In John's gospel, the one who finally persuades individuals to believe the Scriptures and discern the love of God's new family is Jesus himself. The most vigorous argument in the world today is made directly by his presence.

The Persuasive Presence at the Well

"Sir, give me this water, so I will not be thirsty nor come all the way here to draw."

His face remains impenetrable. "Go, call your husband and come here."

The woman's fingers go white around her pot. Water from its wet lip builds against her knuckle, then slips down the back of her hand, slides past her wrist, and finally hangs from her elbow under her sleeve. "I have no husband."

The rabbi's face springs to life—his chin rising, lines appearing on his forehead, his mouth pulling into a benign smile, his eyes narrowing. "You have correctly said, 'I have no husband'; for you have had five husbands, and the one whom you now have is not your husband; this you have said truly."

Another drip races down the woman's arm. *If you knew my past, then why have you been talking to me? Why did you offer me the gift of God?* The woman says nothing.

So the rabbi narrates her life.[2] He recounts her awe of the Samaritan priests and elders as a child, her love of their prayers, her thrill at the sound of their chants. He recounts the gentleness of the man to whom she was betrothed, barely out of childhood. He enumerates the man's promises. Then he tells of her husband's secret insults when she lay exposed in front of him, the lies he told the priest and the scribe. The rabbi repeats the word *indecent*, which her husband used to label her, and describes the certificate her husband gave her before throwing her out of his house.

The rabbi recounts the way the priest averted his eyes whenever she met him in the street.

A second husband rescued her, and the rabbi recounts his gentleness and his promises, and then his insults and his lies. The rabbi tells about how she was more pleased by adultery with a third man than she ever was from marriage. And on and on, relentlessly, and yet with pinpoint accuracy, with wisdom, distinguishing the wrongs done to her from the wrongs she did—first in her thoughts, then in her plans, then in her deeds.

She knew how much she needed living water. But this was different. Now she knew that *the rabbi knew how much she needed it*. His knowledge of her was comprehensive, his judgments effortless. And his knowledge of her was clearer than her knowledge of herself. He could get that knowledge from only one source. God, the same God who, according to the rabbi, offers her a gift.

"Sir, I perceive that you are a prophet. What does God say about where one should worship Him? Our fathers worshiped in this mountain. But you know what their priests and their traditions have done to me—and you know what I have done. Am I supposed to go back to them and worship?

And you Jews say that in Jerusalem is the place where men ought to worship. But your priests won't let me worship there."

The rabbi leans toward her, his voice dropping. "Woman, believe me, an hour is coming when neither in this mountain nor in Jerusalem will you worship the Father."

Her eyes freeze on his.

"You Samaritans worship what you do not know. You know Yahweh, the great I AM, but you have never heard that he is the fountain of living waters. Your fathers ignore the prophets because the prophets do not uphold your fathers' traditions. Your fathers have not taught you any of Yahweh's plans, anything about Messiah, the Son of David, anything about the outpouring of his Spirit on all people.

"We worship what we know, for salvation is from the Jews. We have not only the law, but the prophets as well. Those prophets tell of the hour that is coming, and now is, when the true worshipers will worship the Father in spirit and truth. They will have the fountain of living waters welling up in their own souls, and they will fulfill the righteousness of the law with new hearts. The Father seeks such people to worship him according to his own nature, in spirit and in truth."

The woman searches her memory. What the rabbi describes is like the Prophet who Moses predicted would come. But the rabbi is right: what little her fathers taught about the Prophet was vague at best. The rabbi sits back and waits, while she looks at her pot. The woman looks at him again. "We know—"

He still waits, his face now impassive and his eyes like those of the magistrate—his eyes refusing even to hint at what the correct reply might be. *He is ruthless, this rabbi. Does he seriously expect me to decide this matter on my own?* Her eyes drop back to her pot. "I know—"

"Woman, what do you know?"

"I know that Messiah is coming (he who is called the Christ); when that one comes, he will declare all things to us."[3]

The rabbi's lips pull again into a small smile. "I AM, who speak to you."[4]

The Persuasive Presence Now

Evangelicals seem conflicted about Jesus speaking today.

We say that he speaks. Of course he speaks. Of course he's risen from the dead. Of course the Holy Spirit is active in the world.

But the matters of how he speaks and what role believers have in his speaking—those matters send evangelicals running in all directions.

Many conservative evangelicals emphasize that Jesus speaks through Scripture. Most note that the Spirit plays a role in biblical preaching, but then they teach verses as if they were mere lists of words that require definition, as if the drier the bones of their outlines the more obvious the Spirit's power will be. Other conservatives actually emphasize the Spirit, expressing a longing for revival. But this longing often reduces to despair that the Spirit seems not to "move" anymore. Among biblically focused believers generally, talk of Jesus speaking today is resisted as so much mysticism.

More common is the embrace of the supernatural in Pentecostalism. The immediate presence of Jesus and the work of the Spirit is emphasized almost exclusively. But often the intellectual rigors of studying the Scriptures are openly scorned. There is not a culture of scholarly discipline in Pentecostal churches because the life of the mind is seen as dry and dead— and they are thinking of conservative preaching.

The most common ethos among evangelicals is the marginalization of both the Scriptures and the Spirit. The marketing executives in pulpits are all about buy-in. They are focused on immediate incentives, strong brand identity, and systems to produce results. This agenda does not permit the laborious process of teaching texts. It creates malls rather than organic communities and leaves no room in the communication process for Jesus to speak—leaves nothing to "chance." The supernatural work of God is what happens when we're done with our programs.[5]

But John's gospel is clear. Jesus is the one who persuades the world— Jesus personally. He is not persuasive in the sense that he is a product that sells itself. The coherence of biblical doctrine about him is not the compelling force that gains people's faith. Even the community of believers, as potent a demonstration of love as it can be, does not finally shine the light in the darkness. Jesus personally, actively persuades.

Here's another way to say the same thing. Jesus wasn't making a series of memorable points to the Samaritan woman—though what he said was memorable. He wasn't correcting her theology—though it was corrected. He wasn't luring her with a hopeful vision for her future—though she seized hope. Jesus gave the Samaritan woman himself.

Evangelicals seem to be reluctant to shine a spotlight on the resurrected Jesus. I hear them make argument after argument, pushing with a harder and harder sell. But, more than any of this content, I hear them preaching their own anxiety, as if their broken-heartedness will persuade the darkness to relent. To my ear, this garrulous anxiety speaks louder than their arguments. They seem to be afraid that if they shine the spotlight on Jesus, he won't show.

The Samaritan woman demonstrates the power of testimony. She testifies to the men of Sychar, "Come, see a man" (4:29). She shines the spotlight on a person. This man could be the Christ, a reference to a scriptural concept that her fellow Samaritans knew, if only partially. She is so bold as to make a connection between this man and the Scriptures because he "told me all the things that I have done." Her personal experience of him matched what she knew of the Scriptures. She leaves it up to Jesus to speak for himself. And after the Samaritans spend two days with Jesus, they tell her, "It is no longer because of what you said that we believe, for we have heard for ourselves and know that this One is indeed the Savior of the world" (4:42).

> **Testimony**: An account that focuses attention on Jesus Christ.

In engaging the individuals of the diversity culture, then, we have a definite role. We give them testimony by connecting the Scriptures and our experiences, we take them to a community that has witnessed the same connections, and we tell them that all of this truth-in-life comes from a living man. If we give them this complete testimony, we know that Jesus himself will speak to them.

BECOMING A HEALER: PREPARE YOUR TESTIMONY

- Recall an experience in which Jesus Christ spoke directly to your conscience, as he did to the Samaritan woman. Write a detailed description of how you saw him.
- Select Scriptures that played a role in your experience and incorporate them into your testimony. "What I saw matched what the Bible described."
- Pray diligently for more direct experiences of the presence of Jesus Christ through his Word.
- Tell someone your experience.
- Repeat this process as often as possible.

Part 3

APPLY THE MODEL

8

BE A HERETIC

He lives on a tugboat in Sausalito, California. He is building the world's slowest computer in Nevada, a clock engineered to run for ten thousand years from temperature changes inside a mountain. He's been at least a decade ahead of major technological and cultural changes for forty years. He is the subject of two new academic studies. And a profile of him spent more than a day on the *Times* most e-mailed list in late February, 2007.

"An Early Environmentalist, Embracing New 'Heresies'" by John Tierney surveyed the eccentric career and opinions of Stewart Brand.[1]

The diversity culture watches individuals like Brand, who live where subcultures intersect. As we have seen, the patrons of Café Siddhartha have a temperamental aversion to being put in a box, and they habitually mix their status symbols. We have also seen that, because they rarely inherit a specific culture, they have fluid, self-invented identities. So their attraction to individuals with baroque personal histories is partly a matter of personal identification.

But it is also a matter of trust. Those who have broader experiences are better able to interpret new developments in society.

Many in the diversity culture think that the narrow, complacent middle class rarely escapes its boxed life, rarely sees what happens in the messy world beyond. The picket-fenced people cannot identify with the experiences of others, cannot envision life past the horizons of mortgages and soccer, cannot think for themselves. They are merely the clones of the consumer society, so when they open their mouths, the diversity culture closes its ears. Narrowness of experience is not trustworthy.

I think the diversity culture's critique of the middle class has some merit. The individual who lives at an intersection of subcultures sees more of what's happening. I know a church consultant who works with every brand of Christian from Episcopalian to the Church of God. He gets to see what lots of groups are doing. I know musicians who play both classical and jazz. They see what's happening among musicians of many styles. Café Siddhartha understands this dynamic and wants to hear from the people who take in the most territory. Individuals with a view of the intersection can see the onset of change better than anyone else.

And Stewart Brand is a Grand Central Station of subcultures.

Begin with Ken Kesey's Merry Pranksters, the counterculture group made famous by Tom Wolfe's book *The Electric Kool-Aide Acid Test* in the 1960s. Brand was on the LSD bus, directing multimedia shows at the Pranksters' acid tests. But he was more than the typical enthusiast for psychedelia. Tierney says that Brand designed the shows "drawing on the cybernetic theories of Norbert Wiener, the M.I.T. mathematician who applied principles of machines and electrical networks to social institutions." Not many people can put acid and cybernetic theories together.

That's just the beginning.

Brand started the Whole Earth Catalog, devoted to organic farming and computers. He was one of the founders of The WELL, an early version of the World Wide Web. His digerati connections ran from "the Homebrew Computer Club in the 1970s to *Wired* magazine in the 1990s." And he was an environmentalist. "In 1969, he was so worried by population growth that he organized the Hunger Show, a weeklong fast in a parking lot to dramatize the coming global famine predicted by Paul Ehrlich, one of his mentors at Stanford."

His current environmental views were the prod for Tierney's profile.

Tierney's lead: "Stewart Brand has become a heretic to environmentalism, a movement he helped found, but he doesn't plan to be isolated for long. He expects that environmentalists will soon share his affection for nuclear power. They'll lose their fear of population growth and start appreciating sprawling megacities. They'll stop worrying about 'frankenfoods' and embrace genetic engineering."

How long will this take? Brand thinks ten years, no doubt prompting some to wonder how much acid he took.

Yet when his reasoning emerges, his appraisal acquires a certain inevitability. Nuclear power is cleaner than other electricity-generating options, and its output is enormous. The flight of third-world poor to megacities allows farms to revert to forests. The lower birthrate is not healthy because it will result in too few young people. And genetically engineered crops can use fewer acres and fewer gallons of pesticide.

Brand's brain is a kind of organic forecast of what may happen as American political coalitions on the left and right continue to splinter. The next decade will see an ideological realignment, with groups becoming allies in combinations that today would seem very strange indeed.

Evangelicals tend to monitor the mainstream. Much of the time, they try to understand social changes from within the narrow subculture of the white middle class. The most radical of them read journals on demographics. But they'd understand contemporary changes better if they went to the intersections of cultures and monitored the people who don't fit in neat boxes.

We have considered how to understand the woman at Café Siddhartha. We have analyzed what points of emphasis evangelicals should adopt in their message. Now, we turn to the matter of dialogue. How should evangelicals interact with the woman?

To begin with, they should not only watch the weirdos, the people who don't fit in boxes, but, if they can swing it without acid, they should *become* weirdos. They'd have more credibility.

Weirdo: Someone who does not fit any single subculture to the satisfaction of other people.

The Stubborn Communicator

Look at three moments in John's portrayal of Jesus. The Lord refuses to fit in people's boxes.

In John 2:23–25, the apostle makes a general comment about Jesus' relationship to the masses. He says that around the time Jesus drove the moneychangers from the temple during the Passover, "many believed in His name." They were drawn to him because of "His signs which He was doing." He was gaining a mass following because of the heady mixture of miracles and a corruption-busting message.

But Jesus did not allow himself to be driven by the crowd. As John puts it, he "was not entrusting Himself to them." The words *entrust himself* mean several things at least. Jesus did not regard the mass following as his power base, the source of strength that would enable him to defeat his enemies. He did not allow mass response to shape his message, finding things to say that would keep the crowd in a lather. And he did not blindly accept the crowd's applause as a sincere agreement with his message or a genuine faith in him. The reason was that "He knew all men." John says that Jesus "did not need anyone to testify concerning man, for He Himself knew what was in man." Many dark agendas are masked by a crowd's ambient noise.

This is Jesus the anti-populist. For him, the mass following is not automatically evidence of success. It is a trap. So he does not allow himself to be turned into a symbol easily co-opted by others. He won't be boxed.

John records a specific instance of Jesus' policy toward the crowd.[2] After Jesus feeds five thousand men from five loaves and two fish (6:5–14), the crowd says, "This is truly the Prophet who is to come into the world." But Jesus does not trust the pious buzz. Instead, he makes his own assessment of what the crowd wants, "perceiving that they were intending to come and take Him by force to make Him king" (6:15). In other words, Jesus has a cool head for analyzing his popularity and forecasting where his popularity will take him. We aren't told how he makes this assessment, whether it's through his eyes and ears or through prophecy, but John is clear that this sort of judgment call is basic to Jesus' decision-making.

Once Jesus perceives the crowd's agenda, he "withdrew again to the mountain by Himself alone." John is emphatic about Jesus' isolation. Jesus doesn't only *withdraw* from the crowd, nor only withdraw *by himself.* He withdraws by himself *alone.* Jesus isolates himself even from the giddiness of his disciples, leaving them to get blown about on the Sea of Galilee by a storm.

For Jesus, to fulfill the expectations of the group, to climb into the correct box, is to compromise his mission. His intimate unity with the Father requires him to be singular.

If Jesus' policy against being labeled applies to his so-called friends, it certainly applies to his enemies. When Pilate interrogates him about the Jewish leaders' charges (18:33–38), Pilate asks about Rome's central concern: "Are You the King of the Jews?"

Consider the visceral reaction this question could have provoked in Jesus. He was the embodiment of Psalms 2 and 110, prophecies of his royalty and dominion triumphant against all opposition. His own people were rebelling against him, the people to whom he gave the land, the law, and the promise of the kingdom. He was interrogated in his own capitol about his identity, as if he were some con artist, as if the greedy hypocrites in charge of his nation actually had authority over him. These very same hypocrites would disown their Lord and proclaim their allegiance to Caesar (19:15). And he was asked about his kingship by a foreign emperor's proxy, the regent of one of the kings of the earth who conspired against him.

He had good reason to answer Pilate's question with scorn. The one who sits in heaven, after all, looks down at haughty rebels and laughs.

In spite of all this truth about his nature and position, Jesus does not answer Pilate directly, but counters with a question of his own: "Are you saying this on your own initiative or did others tell you about Me?" (18:34). This move shows two things about Jesus. First, it shows that he is aware of the many different connotations of the phrase *King of the Jews.* To Jews generally, it stands for both worldly and theological realities. To those who are trying to kill him, the phrase is nothing but bait for the insecurities of

Caesar's procurator (19:12). For the procurator himself, the phrase is equal to treason. Jesus will not use a phrase about himself when its significance is unclear. Second, Jesus' counterquestion to Pilate shows that he does not toss information about himself around without making a precise assessment of his audience. Until Pilate reveals his own mind about the information he has received, or changes the terms of the question, Jesus will not declare himself.

Pilate reacts to Jesus' hauteur from the gut: "I am not a Jew, am I? Your own nation and the chief priests delivered You to me; what have You done?" (18:35). But behind the bluster, Pilate has broadened the question, allowing Jesus to answer on his own terms. Pilate no longer asks, "Are You the King of the Jews?" but, "What have You done?"

Now Jesus gives Pilate exactly the information he needs to know: "My kingdom is not of this world." Almost "yes, I am a king," but not quite. His kingdom is in a reality beyond the earthly. Jesus offers an indisputable fact to show that the distinction he makes between this world and another world is genuine. "If My kingdom were of this world, then My servants would be fighting so that I would not be handed over to the Jews; but as it is, My kingdom is not of this realm" (18:36). Without directly calling himself a king, Jesus tells Pilate that his reign offers no competition to Caesar's.

Pilate moves to clarify (18:37). "So You are a king?" Jesus allows the term *king* to stand as Pilate's description. "You said it." But Jesus elaborates his own description of himself. "For this I have been born, and for this I have come into the world, to testify to the truth. Everyone who is of the truth hears My voice." Jesus speaks in theological terms, demonstrating to Pilate that the dispute between Jesus and the Jewish leaders is religious.

Jesus exhibits a conscious strategy in John's gospel, one of giving out information exclusively on his own terms. He cannot make himself understood by fitting easily into existing boxes.

The Winning Communicator

As we've seen, the Samaritan woman has a street philosophy that enables her to interact with strangers, even when there is the potential for hostility. She lives in a culture that, for its time, is diverse and unstable. So when Jesus asks her for a drink, she tests him.

She first tests him on the matter of religion and ethnicity. "How is it that You, being a Jew, ask me for a drink since I am a Samaritan woman?" (4:9). You obviously don't have the typical Jewish agenda. So what *is* your ethnic code? Are you really outside of that box? Jesus' answer, as we've observed, not only evades the Jewish-Samaritan conflict, but even assumes the two cultures are irrelevant (4:10). If she had an accurate understanding of him, she would ask him for the gift of God.

> **Test**: A way to establish that a person can or cannot be trusted.

The woman won't let the matter of culture drop easily (4:11–12). How will Jesus get living water without a bucket? "You are not greater than our father Jacob, are You, who gave us the well, and drank of it himself and his sons and his cattle?" The woman's test here has more push-back than before. She brings up the inflammatory issues of lineage and property, the Samaritan claim to belong to God's people through Joseph's line and therefore to own the well at Sychar. She deliberately tries to provoke Jewish suspicion about Samaritan shiftiness. Again, Jesus escapes being put in that box (4:13–14). He isn't talking about this water, which only leaves people thirsty, but about the fountain of eternal life.

The woman's final test is the most emotionally exposed (4:19–20). After Jesus has revealed her sins, where does he say she should worship in order to find God's gift of living water? She has no hope on Mt. Gerizim, and she is excluded from the temple in Jerusalem. At this moment, she raises issues just as inflammatory as the legacy of Jacob. But she raises them not out of curiosity, but from the perspective of immediate need, and she requires an outside-the-box answer. Jesus escapes being boxed once more (4:21–24). "Woman, believe Me, an hour is coming when neither in this mountain nor in Jerusalem will you worship the Father."

Each of these tests went into visceral territory for a Jewish man. The fact that Jesus controlled his reactions and made replies that were outside the usual categories was not just a tactical coup. His heresies against his Jewish ethnicity were the foundation of his credibility with the Samaritan woman. John shows us Jesus' navigation of the cultural issues so we can see how he defused hostility and opened ears.

The Ear-Opening Communicator

Consider David Brooks's three guides to the maze of Flexidoxy: *Don't be certain. Don't be a hero. Don't be a critic.* Each of these statements prompts a visceral reaction from many evangelicals, an eruption of argument to show . . . what, exactly?

Don't be certain? I am certain! God says it. I believe it. That settles it. Jesus is the way, the truth, and the life.

Don't be a hero? We could use a few heroes! We need people who'll take a stand, who'll say there's right and wrong, and who won't back down even if the cost is steep. We need people who'll shake things up.

Don't be a critic? You can't look at our culture and not criticize it. It's rotten to the core. We don't have any values anymore. The public schools aren't educating kids, just filling them with a lot of New Age garbage. Hollywood is polluting people's imaginations with filth. It's about time we got some critics.

I hear many evangelicals take their stand on slogans and generalizations, hoping to show strength and conviction. But if the Baptist at Café Siddhartha makes any one of the above statements, the woman will put him in the box of vainglorious fanaticism. He will prove that he views the world from a narrow vantage point and that he can only spout prepackaged sentiments. He will not be credible.

The Baptist might console himself with pious self-talk, like the line that he's been faithful to declare the truth and isn't accountable for results. But the standard for faithfulness is Jesus' methods, which involved a high sensitivity to the perceptions of his audience. A Christian can only consider himself to have been faithful when he has met Jesus' standard.

The consoling self-talk might take a more theological form: hard-hearted sinners will never accept the truth, no matter how nicely you dress it up. But not even "the righteous" should accept slogans as truth. The key to speaking the truth is its application. Truth is "a word spoken in right circumstances," a word that impresses its listeners like fine craftsmanship, like "apples of gold in settings of silver" (Prov. 25:11). Truth is not a generalization that satisfies the speaker. A Christian can only claim to have given out the truth when he has crafted his words to fit his hearer's life.

Still, as I keep noting, our story on the Baptist may be wrong. He could well be effective the way Jesus was, being able to evade boxes. The Baptist may not use the slogans we think he'll use. He may be faithful by actually meeting Jesus' standard of sensitivity and applying truth with precision.

Here is my strategy for evading boxes. In any dialogue about spiritual things, I apply a biblical truth that my listener does not expect.

Consider each of Brooks's three guides again.

Don't be certain. Many images are projected onto the word *certainty*, and I am just as inclined to reject them as the woman at Café Siddhartha. The stadium full of fervent Hitler youth. The fervent scientist who refuses to admit any role in life for spirituality. The fervent believer in prayer who is certain she must not use the technology of modern medicine. A person of any sense at all, Christian or non-Christian, is suspicious of fervency that refuses to acknowledge questions.

My friend Dave is an ex-philosophy major, and one day he described a documentary he'd seen called *Jesus Camp.* It showed a Pentecostal summer camp that whipped children into a frenzy to reach America for Christ. Dave's voice was getting tighter, his gestures more rigid, and he pointed his index finger at my nose. "That's why people hate religion—the bogus certainty."

I felt all the tension of defensiveness. I focused on that phrase *bogus certainty* and instinctively wanted to show that my certainty was anything but bogus. I was also nagged by an inner voice that said, "Don't betray your brethren in Christ. Stick up for them!"

But I nodded at Dave's challenge. "You're right. That camp is just emotionally manipulating those kids." It was what I really thought. So I said it.

Dave's shoulders relaxed. "Exactly."

"Our church runs a camp for kids too. But we teach them to question what they hear."

"You what?"

"We teach them to question what they hear. We teach them that God speaks directly to them in the Bible, and that they can study it for themselves to find out what they need to do. Frankly, Dave, I don't study the Bible because I'm certain, but because I'm uncertain. I don't know anyone I can trust with my spiritual life. I have to trust God."[3]

Dave's ears opened.

Don't be a hero. Again, there are many negative images that street postmodernism projects onto the word *hero,* and I have no interest in defending them. The raw recruit who's eager to go to war. The demagogic politician who manipulates the crowd. The crusading moralist. I do feel that spiritual heroism is needed today, but it cannot be a heroism of credulity.

Later in my conversation with Dave about *Jesus Camp,* we talked about the emotional manipulation he saw in the film. He specifically reacted to the speakers who created a sense of national doom to drive children to tears. Dave asked, "Why do those preachers work kids over that way? I mean, that's abusive."

I nodded. "It is abusive. Preachers have a lot of power over people's emotions, and using that power week in and week out can give them big egos. They can become the heroes of their own sermons, and they can feel justified in saying anything to get results." I told him that solid spiritual decisions don't come from an intense emotional experience, but from a conscious process of change. "Working people over emotionally is just a cheap gimmick. As far as I'm concerned, my job as a preacher is to disappear behind Jesus' message. That usually means I have to be calm."

Dave's ears opened more.

Don't be a critic. Once more, there are negative images that go with the word *critic*, images that I don't want to embrace. The angry white male. The preacher to the choir. The fault-finding hypocrite, whose sins are less heinous than everyone else's. I find that I can get more truth across by describing how I remove the log from my own eye than by criticizing others.

I once preached a series called "Jesus and Organized Religion," which we advertised in a local alternative newspaper. One evening, a gay friend of mine mentioned that he'd been following my sermon titles in each weekly ad. "I'm curious about what you're teaching. But I'm also not sure I want to know."

As we stood staring at a crack in the sidewalk, my stomach secreted powerful nausea-inducing agents. *He's asking me not to comment on his lifestyle. Am I allowed to talk to him about the gospel without addressing homosexuality?* I figured I had about twenty words. "We're talking about how institutions often put themselves between individuals and God."

Silence, then a quietly surprised, "Hmm." He looked up from the sidewalk. "So, are you saying this is a bad thing?"

"Yeah. We believe individuals have direct access to God. When institutions put up barriers, they abuse people."

More silence while he returned his gaze to the sidewalk, then another cadential, "Hmm." He now spoke slowly. "Would you say your church puts up barriers, or would you say other churches do it?"

"Other churches do it, and we do it too. That's why I'm preaching this series. For instance, our church is still pretty rural, so there's a sense that you have to conform to the group's ways in order to belong. It's a subtle thing. We wouldn't put that barrier up consciously. But the barrier's still there, and I think we can take it down."

"Why would your church change?"

"Because we really believe that Jesus transforms a person's soul. We've personally seen him move us away from our sins. We know from experience that no one stands between us and Jesus, and we want to get out of Jesus' way."

My friend's ears opened.

In each of these examples, I referred to a biblical teaching that my friends did not expect: I study the Bible because I am suspicious of human wisdom; it's not my job to be the congregation's hero; our church needs to lower some barriers to Jesus. I didn't expect these statements to be the miraculous comebacks that would lead my friends to Christ. I only expected that they would open my friends' ears, and provide a solid foundation for later dialogue.

Some caveats.

Doing or saying the unexpected is not enough to open people's ears to Jesus. The unexpected things we say must be biblical. We need to show that Jesus himself is unexpected, that people should give him another look. If we are evading boxes merely to gain sympathy for ourselves, we'll probably succeed, but without drawing others any closer to Jesus.

Also, the unexpected biblical teachings we show must *actually be biblical*. There is always pressure to redefine the faith so that it fits ungodly prejudices better. For instance, some are experimenting again with the notion that people of other faiths will be saved as long as they are sincere. Some others want to blur biblical standards on sexuality so that we seem less prudish. None of these faux-biblical teachings will lead people to Jesus.

Finally, there will be times to say things that open us to slander and mockery. Jesus calls us to do no less. He was impaled on the cross for exactly such uncompromising stands.

But Jesus did not hand his enemies the hammers and nails.

BECOMING A HEALER: SELF-CONTROL

- We all have things we say over and over about political, spiritual, or moral issues. We have a standard speech. Ask your spouse or a close friend what your standard speech is.
- What resentments animate your standard speech? What evil are you trying to correct?
- Suppose you could never give your standard speech again. What would you say about political, spiritual, or moral issues instead? How would you open people's ears?

9

FIND YOUR MODE

John Humphrys, a prominent host on the BBC's Radio 4, did a series of interviews about faith in 2006 called "Humphrys in Search of God," which generated an astounding response in Britain. After the series ended, he wrote, "I had thousands of replies and, four months after the broadcasts, they're still coming."[1] A reviewer for the *Daily Telegraph*, Gillian Reynolds, summed up Humphrys' approach. "Brought up as a Christian, for 50 years he has found it impossible to believe in God. In conversations with three religious leaders, he invites them to convince him otherwise, to convert him."[2]

Humphrys explained his personal crisis in an essay for the *Telegraph*. "I was finding it increasingly difficult to reconcile the God to whom I had been introduced at Sunday school with the reality of the world I was told he had created."[3] So, he wrote, he focused the interviews on the problem of evil, asking religious leaders such as Dr. Rowan Williams, the Archbishop of Canterbury, how God could permit horrors such as the massacre of children by Chechen terrorists at Beslan or the death of a colleague after a battle with cancer.

Of the thousands of letters he received in response, many came from British evangelicals trying to convert him—so many, in fact, that Humphrys wondered why Britain's churches were empty. He commented on the letters, "They make it sound so simple. All I have to do, it seems, is open my heart to Jesus and that's it. I will see the light and my life will never be the same again. I hate to sound cynical but this rather misses the point."[4] Humphrys was stuck on a contradiction he saw in prayer, that "God is either interventionist or He is not. If He answers our prayers, then He clearly is. But if He allows free will, He is not."[5] A simplistic leap of faith such as the evangelicals were calling him to make was not an answer to the issue he faced.

While John Humphrys does not precisely reflect the conflict between evangelicals and the diversity culture in America, he may offer a glimpse into the American future. In twenty years, it is possible that most Americans will be hardened in agnosticism while churches stand empty and evangelicals huddle in enclaves. Humphrys epitomizes what evangelicals find intimidating about patrons of Café Siddhartha—their intellectualism, their anticipation of pat answers, their rhetorical smackdowns. The prospect of having to deal personally with a John Humphrys is what evangelicals dread about an agnostic-dominated culture. But he also shows the potential openings that evangelicals miss because they are stuck in a defensive crouch.

Is Humphrys as closed as he appears?

Notice Your Approach

I find that there are two modes of dialogue with people in the diversity culture.

There's the ideological mode. This is the mode in which we talk about Barack Obama and the economy, gay marriage, and creationists in Kansas. Ideological mode is all about scoring points. You have to know your facts, be deadly with sarcasm, and be quick to spot weaknesses. You see the boxes that your opponent wants to put you in, and instead of evading them, you fortify them. You dare your opponent to bust your bulwark. In this mode, your invented self either intimidates your opponent or offers him a clear shot at your head.

Ideological Mode: A debate characterized by attack, defense, and spin.

It's a game. It's fun.

Some evangelicals make the mistake of trying to use ideological mode to communicate the gospel. For them, it's all about having answers, piling up evidence, proving points. They're stuck using the reject-correct approach we saw in chapter 4. Others see the futility of trying to argue people into the kingdom, but nevertheless are nagged by a sense of duty: fight the futile battle or else you're disloyal. Still others think the people of Café Siddhartha can be won to Christ if evangelicals openly adopt their ideology: oppose the Iraq war, be green, etc. Thus, some who use the accept-affirm approach from chapter 4 are in ideological mode too.

But the gospel raises issues that are too deep to be discussed in the context of positioning and spin.

From what we've seen of Jesus and the Samaritan woman, he was not in ideological mode. He wasn't going to let himself be defined by cultural conflicts. He wasn't going to argue with the woman about who owned Jacob's well or give lectures about history and theology. But neither was he going to ingratiate himself by turning to the Samaritan side. He was in another mode of dialogue entirely.

The other mode is relational. In this mode, there is no competition. There are no points to score. The subjects we discuss have to do with life—hopes, fears, disappointments,

> **Relational Mode**: A discussion characterized by trust, openness, and often risk.

yearnings, experiences. This mode has uncompromising standards. You must let your guard down, because your invented self, with all its calculation and artifice, is a liability. You must listen. You must be able to think clearly from multiple points of view. You must be willing to get hurt. But adhering to these standards has a big payoff, because this is the mode that enables two people to share their souls.

Most of the evangelicals who use the accept-affirm approach at Café Siddhartha are trying to stay in relational mode. They want to keep ideology out of the dialogue, and to that extent they are right. But they do not engage others wisely. Because they accept and affirm indiscriminately, they end up being more altered by the relationship than the person they are trying to win.

So here's a twist. It is possible to discuss political, theological, and moral disagreements in relational mode. It's not just possible, it's normal. For instance, relational mode is where people discuss a movie and its themes: they trade observations, favorite scenes, and criticisms of the acting. Even though moral and intellectual themes may be part of the discussion, there is no pretense that one person will win and the other will lose. Rather, friends discuss the themes in the context of their personal experiences, fears, and yearnings. The deeper the movie, the further that discussion will go.

Jesus is our model for dialogue about spiritual issues relationally. He knew that the Samaritan woman would begin the encounter ideologically. But he shifted the dialogue into relational mode so that they could discuss spiritual issues outside of a win/lose scenario. For evangelicals, encounters at Café Siddhartha will often begin the same way—with the other person's defenses up. Evangelicals must make the same shift Jesus made.

His evasion of the boxes she wanted to put him in, as we discussed in chapter 8, was key to this shift. The woman couldn't write Jesus off as another Jewish rabbi after he asked her for water. She couldn't dismiss his teaching after he ignored an opportunity to set her straight about Jacob's true heirs. She had to relate to him on more personal terms. Still, important as evading her boxes was, Jesus did not finally shift her into a relational dialogue until he revealed his knowledge of her five husbands and her fornication. That surprise was what finally got the woman to drop her defenses. As we have seen, she brought up the issue of where to worship as an expression of her immediate need.

There are two principles we can draw from Jesus' model.

First, the shift out of ideological mode occurs when you hear about a person's crucible. As we saw in chapter 4, people like George Trow get melted down by life's trials, and in the process they learn truths that really are true. If Jesus had not addressed the Samaritan woman's crucible of divorce, their dialogue would never have gone deep enough to expose her need for Jesus' living water. In the same way, we will not succeed in communicating the gospel at the ideological level. We must earn access to an individual's past, to the history of how her experiences taught her to think. If we're talking about her crucible, we're really talking.

True, Jesus had the benefit of prophecy. He could spring his knowledge on the Samaritan woman rather than going through the painstaking process of listening, questioning, and learning. But this point just elevates the importance of our relational skills.

The second principle we can draw from Jesus' model is that the two modes of dialogue must not be mixed.

No one likes a political argument that gets personal. The game-playing element of spin is what keeps antagonists from ripping each other's throats out. It's how avatars of political ideologies such as William F. Buckley and John Kenneth Galbraith could mock each other in a public debate one day, and the next go skiing together in Gstaad. By the same token, no one wants to open up a closely held fear or yearning only to be hit with an ideological taunt. If you mix these two modes of dialogue, you will deserve people's hostility.

Jesus got away with unveiling the Samaritan woman's past because he had been relational all the way through their dialogue. It didn't matter how many ideological tests she might have thrown at him. Jesus would have responded to each one in the relational mode. His credibility lay in his refusal to make the convenient oversimplification, to repeat the party line, to take the cheap shot. He had earned her trust.

Watch Your Impact

The typical evangelical approach to agnostics can be found in the letters that left John Humphrys so irritated. Just pray the prayer. Quit asking all these questions. You're thinking too much. Humphrys brushed off his evangelical correspondents because their generalizing "rather misses the point"—a point he found in another large stack of letters.

These other writers were deeply troubled by the world we're living in and were looking for reasons to believe that God has an active part in it. They were like him, Humphrys said, in that they once had faith, had lost it, and now wanted it back. He referred to one letter from a woman who had cancer. "She lost her faith some years ago and wants a 'heavenly Father to help me at this time.'" She did not find any help or encouragement from the religious leaders Humphrys interviewed in his series. Beneath her signature on the letter, she wrote, "Quite angry really."[6]

Contrast the two types of letters.

A letter that argues with the theology of the Archbishop of Canterbury, pointing out all the inadequacies of his answers to Humphrys' questions, is in ideological mode. A letter filled with rhetorical questions about the state of Humphrys' heart and with attacks on his biased interviewing techniques is also in ideological mode. If that letter closes with an appeal to Humphrys to give his heart to Jesus, it mixes the ideological with the relational in a way that can only be taken as insulting.

But a letter that shares an agonizing cancer story, opens up a yearning for a heavenly Father, and expresses anger at not finding any answers, is squarely in relational mode.

Humphrys' *Telegraph* essay about his radio series, in my opinion, was not ideological. He adopted a strong point of view, and the points he made were often sharp. But he also showed an emotional openness that told me he was looking for solutions to real problems. He didn't have to say that he was trying to recover his faith. In British culture today, it's far more usual to say good riddance to it.

About the interviews themselves, Reynolds commented that his style was like another series of his: "Anyone who has listened to Humphrys in On the Ropes, the series he has done for years on Radio 4 of interviews with people who've come through times that might have broken them, knows that he can be patient, thoughtful, understanding, empathetic when trying to share the experience of being in their shoes."[7] The BBC continues to promote "Humphrys in Search of God" on its Web site by saying that he talks about "his unfulfilled desire to believe in God."[8]

Humphrys exhibited a quality that I admire in many agnostics—emotional honesty.

The evangelical letters failed to communicate with Humphrys because they were ideological. They worked against him, not with him.

Deepen Your Engagement

One afternoon, a man drove a hundred miles to ask some questions.

Ted was an agnostic who had heard a couple of my sermons on CD, passed along by his daughter. She knew of his spiritual struggles and asked if I would be willing to meet with him in the unlikely event he was interested. I said certainly, imagining that a meeting, if it took place at all, would be in the remote future.

I was stunned when Ted made an appointment a couple days later.

When he sat in my office, he went right to his questions—and over the years he had compiled quite a list. One after another, he gave a broad selection of the intellectual problems that often plague agnostics, his eyes darting around the room, his hands rarely still, and his breathing labored. One problem focused on whom Cain married after he was exiled by God for murdering Abel. If Adam and Eve were the only people around, where did this other population come from?

I volunteered the Spencer Tracy line from *Inherit the Wind*. "Did God pull off a creation in the next county?"

Ted looked at me with his eyebrows raised, and then smiled. "Exactly."

I leaned back in my office chair and bounced on the spring. "So, you've probably raised these issues with a lot of people."

He looked aside and addressed his answer to my bookshelf. He had been a Christian for many years, and a committed one. He attended church regularly and respected his pastors. But these questions began to wear on him, and he started to ask his pastors about them. Their answers ticked him off. Mostly, they recommended books such as *The Purpose-Driven Life*, which he would read and find to be badly off-topic.

He concluded that the pastors didn't want to answer his questions.

"I'm sad to say it, Ted, but you may be right. When I was younger, I had a hard time getting answers to my questions from Christians. I mostly got the sense that my questions weren't really important."

"Exactly!" Now Ted was looking at me. More of his story emerged: a church fight, depression, marital conflict.

A crucible was in there somewhere. Through the whole conversation, I felt that he was not yet describing the fire that had changed him, that he was only showing me a few burn scars. I also felt that I needed to wait before probing too deeply into his experiences, that pushing too far in a first conversation would not be respectful.

I thought it was time to offer some intellectual engagement now that we were definitely in relational mode. I circled back to his question about Cain's wife. "You know, Moses was a good storyteller. He didn't repeat stuff unless it was really important."

"Oh?"

"Yeah. He tells us in Genesis 1 that God commanded Adam and Eve to multiply. We're not sure how much time went by before Cain murdered Abel, but Moses wants us to assume that they *were* multiplying. Cain married someone from that population."

Ted thought for a while. "That's the most common-sense thing I've ever heard."

As far as I know, he isn't back in the faith. Maybe I won't get the opportunity to hear Ted's crucible. But if he ever drives that hundred miles again, we'll have a relationship to build on.

There are two things that encourage me when I consider that relationship.

First, Ted took many risks with me, traveling a long distance and sharing many personal experiences. Now, whenever I take risks in conversation, I go back over the exchanges again and again. I think about what I said, the tone I used, the replies I got, the facial expressions the other person made while I was talking. I remember the weird pauses, the moments of tension, the moments of evasion, and I try to understand what caused them. I'm confident that, if I review my risky conversations, Ted probably reviews his too, going back over what I said and how I said it. In other words, I don't have to wonder whether I "got a hearing."

Second, in that conversation, Ted heard me identify with several of his difficult experiences. But he also knew that I still believe, still pray, still trust God. He knew this even though I didn't say it in so many words. The simple fact that I wrestle with similar problems without losing my faith is part of my testimony to him about the resurrected Jesus.

I am not saying that this kind of dialogue—talking with a person about his crucible—is enough. I'm not saying that people will convert just because we take a softer approach. But I am saying that the relational mode is a powerful tool. I am saying that Jesus used it. I am saying that it opens ears. Critical questions can be addressed *more effectively* if we are not competitive with people. I'm also saying that this tool is good, that it gives a blessing. In order to be like Jesus, we have to stop making points at people and start finding points with people.

Demonstrate Your Love

One Sunday, after I preached about Jesus and the woman at the well, my friend Carol told me about her coworker Joan. "She's driven everyone away. She sits alone at her desk. No one will eat lunch with her. Our boss won't even talk to her." Carol's eyes moistened. "I don't want to talk to Joan either. She hates Christians." We talked about ways Carol could break out of the box Joan had made for her, simple things like asking Joan to lunch. We also talked about the homework I had given in the sermon: ask people about their community, where they belong.

After a couple weeks, late in the evening, Carol called me. "I did my homework." Her voice was bright. She had been talking with Joan at lunch and told her, "My pastor has been teaching that people need community." That one observation triggered Joan's story of being beaten as a little girl. But there was more. Joan told Carol, "I know God can change people because it happened to my friend." Joan had seen her friend convert to Christ after being abused by her husband. Joan saw her friend genuinely forgive the man, and find peace in her own soul. "I know God can do that. But I'm just not ready."

Carol's voice brightened even more. "And I just listened."

A week later Carol gave me another update in the aisle at church. Joan had told Carol about going to the doctor and hearing that she had high blood pressure. Joan said, "I guess God's trying to tell me something."

The week after that, Carol told me about another conversation. Joan confessed to carrying "thirty years of bitterness."

Carol understood exactly what was happening during these conversations with Joan. For the first time in a long while, Joan was feeling loved.

BECOMING A HEALER: SELF-AWARENESS

- What are the topics of conversation that shift you into ideological mode?
- What is your tone of voice when you're in ideological mode? If uncertain, ask your spouse, your children, or your friends to imitate you.
- If you were to engage people in relational mode on those hot topics, what tone of voice would you use?

10

ANSWER THE QUESTION

If any evangelicals read Patricia Leigh Brown's article "Supporting Boys or Girls When the Line Isn't Clear" after it appeared on December 2, 2006, they were likely filled with anxiety.[1] It certainly touched a nerve with *New York Times* readers, though probably for different reasons. The article remained on the most e-mailed list for four days. It described the efforts of parents and public schools to support children who are believed to be transgendered.

As we have seen, evangelicals have spent decades in a cultural bubble, trying both to communicate with the outside and to make the inside safer. For decades they have seen that the outside culture is headed for disaster. But the worse the outside culture has become, the more evangelicals have patched their bubble. Rather than interact meaningfully with people, rather than listen in depth to their painful experiences, evangelicals have continued to transmit ever more irrelevant messages from within their hermetically sealed environment. The time they should have spent mastering the countercultural arts, they have spent instead trying to increase the range of their transmitters.

So here is another headline confirming the disaster evangelicals foresaw. The medical and educational establishments are increasingly supportive of children who want to be the opposite gender. It is all too easy for

Counterculture: A nonconformist way of life in the midst of the larger culture.

evangelicals to cry, "Woe to us that we lived to see this. How can we reinforce the bubble?"

Here are the details that evangelicals are trained to seize from a story like Brown's.

Reynaldo Almeida, director of a progressive private school in Oakland, is happy about the new openness to transgendered children. "First we became sensitive to two mommies and two daddies. Now it's kids who come to school who aren't gender typical." Evangelicals read: we've slid farther down the slippery slope.

New York City allows people to change their sex on their birth certificates. Brown also reports that Massachusetts, Minnesota, California, New Jersey, and the District of Columbia all define transgendered students' rights and that schools are rapidly trying to eliminate gender stereotypes. An Oakland day school trains teachers to use gender-neutral terms, urging them to line students up not by boys and girls but by the color of their sneakers. The day school's director doesn't want students to feel "boxed in," but wants them to "move back and forth until something feels right." The Los Angeles Unified School District specifies that staff must address students with "a name and pronoun that corresponds to the gender identity." It even wants schools to provide special locker rooms.

This new position down the slope is being fortified legally and administratively. For evangelicals, Brown's article is the story of encroaching totalitarianism, of bureaucrats imposing their values on the people—and that's as far as most evangelicals want to take it. Call your congressman.

The real story outside the bubble is far worse. A government that tried to ramrod the brave new world could be resisted. What we actually face is a culture that *accepts* the brave new world.

Consider the parents profiled in Brown's piece. While evangelicals were patching their bubble, these parents were inheriting a well-developed philosophy for rearing children. They inherited this philosophy the normal way, from their parents and other authority figures like teachers, doctors, social workers, and therapists. When a parent today is confronted with a

child whom the establishment defines as transgendered, there are principles to be applied.

A child, for instance, cannot be expected to control his or her desires.

One boy dressed more and more in feminine clothing. When his mother
asked him to dress as a boy, he became agitated. The mother knew exactly
how to think about this situation. "It just clicked in me. I said, 'You really
want to wear a dress, don't you?'" She and her husband talked with a psy-
chologist, and accepted the new identity when they "observed [the boy's]
newfound comfort with his choice."

The boy was five.

Take another principle. Trying to change children's desires threatens
their self-image.

The father of "a gender-variant third-grader" notes that transgendered
adults all share the characteristic of not being "accepted and understood as
a child." For this father, his child's situation calls for the application of social science. He studies his child's condition, gathering the stories of other
people's experiences and searching for patterns. Having studied the case
histories, he draws the moral. The worst thing you can do is not understand
your child. "You read [the cases] and think, O.K., best to avoid that."

The principle that you must not try to change your child's desires does
have a corollary.

Some propose that you can moderate a child's desires through medica-
tion. Brown writes, "One of the most controversial issues concerns the use
of 'blockers,' hormones used to delay the onset of puberty in cases where it
could be psychologically devastating (for instance, a girl who identifies as a
boy might slice her wrists when she gets a period)." This argument shows a
recognition that a parent cannot allow her child's condition to be out of control. If the problems can be managed, then those options should be explored.

These parents are in agony trying to make their inherited philosophy
work. Says one, "As a parent you're in this complete terra incognita." Another says that as much as they "choreograph" their child's life "there's
still this stomach-clenching fear for your kid." For most of them, the

Judeo-Christian ethic doesn't exist. The models they saw growing up displayed none of it, and many of them were actively taught to disregard it.

These parents are not conspirators in the end of Western civilization; they are the victims.

The immediate question is, how will evangelicals relate to them? The future problem is still more wrenching. In fifteen years, how will they relate to the growing proportion of adults who are lost in confusion about what it means to be male and female?

Relating to them is not optional. And it cannot be done from within a bubble.

Answers Give Comfort

After Jesus gave the Samaritan woman a narrative of her life, she raised the question of worship. We have seen that the issue was the obvious one to bring up. We've also seen that the issue was tangled in ethnic animosity, manipulations of scriptural texts, and literal warfare. She was sunk in deep, even toxic, confusion. Specifically, she raised the conflict over whether true worship occurred at Mt. Gerizim or Jerusalem. The question the woman implied was, "Which place will give me the Father's living water?"

If Jesus' goal had been to defend Israel against Samaritan slanders, then his reply would have been quite different from the one John recorded. He would have attacked the question. Jerusalem and Mt. Gerizim were in no way comparable. The Samaritan priests were frauds. Her ethnic heritage was hopelessly mixed. Her people have shifted from the Lord to idols and back again. Jesus would have said, "God can only be worshiped in Jerusalem," a reply that would have betrayed the trust she had given him up to this point in the dialogue.

But Jesus didn't defend Israel in these ways, much less try to turn the Samaritan woman into an Israelite. He did not converse with her in the mode of ideology. He consistently evaded the label of the "typical rabbi." And he was sensitive to her fluid identity and difficult past.

His goal was to win her to himself.

So he did something that we all do when we care about someone, when we know they are in a struggle, and when we hear them express a deep need for truth. He answered her question. "Woman, believe Me, an hour is coming when neither in this mountain nor in Jerusalem will you worship the Father" (4:21).

His answer had two characteristics we should notice.

It was *direct*. It spoke to the issue exactly the way she raised it. Jesus understood that she was not setting a trap, baiting him for the next item on her agenda, or playing any other ideological game. The woman raised this issue because she needed a solution. So Jesus spoke directly to the problem of worship as she perceived it. To be sure, he expanded on his answer later. His initial *neither* was only a partial response. But it opened the new possibilities she needed.

Often, we fail to answer people's questions because we answer what we perceive to be their agendas. Our story on them, and the stories we're sure they have on us, skew our interpretation of the dialogue. When evolutionary biologist Scott Atran asks why human beings throw away logic to retain their belief in God, we answer by attacking the theory of evolution. *That's what Atran is really about*—never mind that he's been wrestling with this question from childhood. When John Humphrys asks whether God intervenes in earthly events to answer prayer, we attack his interviewing style. *He's just trying to make Christians look bad*—never mind that he too has wrestled with his question for years. In other words, instead of answering people's questions, we reveal our most uncharitable assumptions about their motives. We betray their trust.

In addition to being direct, Jesus' answer to the woman was *focused*. He was not merely responding to her issue, but was continuing to pursue his own goal. His theme through the conversation was that eternal life is beyond the spheres of Samaria and Israel both. That was why he offered her access to the gift of God, why he disregarded the Samaritan-Jewish conflict, why he didn't react when she baited him about Jacob's well. So her question about location advanced his theme.

Put differently, Jesus had an opportunity to show the woman that his agenda and hers matched. She needed living water beyond her well. He wanted her to have that very water. All he had to do was answer the question just the way she asked it.

Answers Gain Trust

The simple act of answering people's questions directly, as if they had no ulterior motives in posing them, is a powerful way to gain trust and defuse tension even without the benefit of a close relationship.

Our congregation collects questions from their non-Christian friends every year, and I choose seven of them to answer in a sermon series. The first year we did this, we received the question, "Why do Christians hate gays?"

There were several ways I could have answered, all of which would've assumed that the question was asked in ideological mode—that it was designed to cause me problems. I could have attacked the assumption of the question. "Christians do not, in fact, hate gays, and I resent the implication that we do." I could also have tried a less confrontational assault on the question's premise. "Christians don't hate the sinners. They hate the sin." Further, I could have assailed the politically correct methodology of defining all moral disagreements in terms of either hate or tolerance.

All of these answers would have been anticipated by unbelievers—especially the shrewd ones, who are legion. The stock answers would have landed me in a box.

Stock Answer: A generalized, prefabricated reply that ends discussion.

So I began the sermon by saying that there are at least three reasons why many Christians hate gays, none of which is excusable. First, many Christians hate gays because they are physically repelled by the gay lifestyle. Second, I said, many Christians hate gays because of gays' higher social status—their money, their careers, their acceptance among the "elites." Third, many Christians hate gays for playing a role in the destruction of America's Judeo-Christian heritage. Not one of these reasons releases Christians from their duty to demonstrate—not just profess—Christlike love.

All the time I was saying these things, my shoulders felt rigid as plywood and my throat was tight, not because I worried that I was wrong, but because I felt exposed and weak. Still, the approach seemed like the most honest way to introduce the principle that we are to be Christ's ambassadors of reconciliation, pleading with gays to be reconciled to God (2 Cor. 5:16–21).

The response was intense, especially from Christian parents of gays, who had felt the sting of the hatred I was describing. Two such couples came to our first service and stayed to hear the sermon a second time. A copy of the sermon found its way to a believing couple in Idaho, whose daughter is a lesbian. The mother wrote a lengthy thank you.

I also got response from a local newspaper even before I preached the sermon. A reporter called me to say that she had heard from four people infuriated by my sermon title ("Why Do Christians Hate Gays?") on our church sign. "You've really offended some people in this community. Is that a responsible thing to do?"

"We collected a number of questions from the community," I answered, "and this question was one of them. The fact that all these questions came from the community has been in all our advertising for the past month. I recognize how provocative the question is, but I felt it would've been dishonest to soften it. I figured I'd better answer it."

The line was silent for a long time. Eventually, she asked, "So do you think hatred of gays is justified?"

"No. It is inexcusable."

A slightly shorter silence. "Well, are gays welcome at your church?"

"Certainly. We welcome everyone for dialogue about how Christ can transform our lives."

More silence. "Okay, well, can a homosexual be a Christian?"

"Anyone can come to Christ for transformation, and Christ will accept that person as he or she is. The Bible teaches that he'll lead them away from their sins and make them more like himself."

For fifteen minutes the reporter threw issue after issue at me. Then said she would interview some other people and call me back with more questions before she wrote her story. After I hung up, I felt drained, anxious, even devastated. I worried that my replies had been foolish and cowardly, wishing I had not done the series at all. But she never called back. The story never ran.

I later learned that she was a lesbian.

Answers Give Affirmation

When I taught the principles that make up this chapter at my church, I felt that using Brown's story about transgender toddlers was risky. Orland is a rural town. The idea of the local schools or county social workers using the concepts Brown described in the *New York Times* might be a stretch. And the notion that some local people actually struggled to cope with children labeled transgendered might seem ridiculous.

Or Brown's story might shock the congregation so badly that, in reacting to the cultural implications of it, they could miss the mandate of compassion.

But I used the story in spite of these concerns, presenting it as something that believers face in California's dreaded Bay Area, three hours down the interstate, and that we'll have to address in Orland at some point in the hazy future.

I said, "Let's suppose that you were friends with one of the parents described in Brown's article. I realize how unlikely it sounds, but just suppose your friend tells you that her five-year-old boy wants to dress like a girl, that a social worker has said the child may be transgendered. She doesn't ask you whether that's right or wrong, or whether the Bible has anything to say about the issue. She asks you how she should build up her son's self-esteem. What do you say?"

I said that, if we're guided by our knee-jerk reactions, *self-esteem* is what we focus on. *How can my friend be distracted by psychobabble at a time like this? That social worker wants her to train the boy in perversity, let him wander into something that will ruin his life before he even sees adolescence. And she's worried about his self-esteem?*

From that perspective, we might answer our friend's question by talking about the depravity of man and the darkness of her son's heart. We might give her all the reasons why she shouldn't trust the social worker—the liberal training, the totalitarian agenda, the false view of sexuality as a purely social construct rather than a biological fact. We might launch a full-scale assault on the concept of self-esteem, and describe the role this concept has played in the decline of Judeo-Christian values.

I said, "We have to take these approaches—right?—because the boy's soul depends on whether we can convince his mother of the truth."

But what if we took another approach? What if we simply answered the question our friend actually asked? How can she build up her son's self-esteem when he's been labeled transgendered?

The Bible has a lot to say about how to nurture children into confident, healthy, and joyful adults. *A lot* to say. What our friend will never be able to achieve using the psychological concept of self-esteem becomes possible if she begins to think about the Bible's teachings for herself.

I proposed redefining our friend's problem using the book of Proverbs. Her son's self-esteem isn't threatened by an issue of gender confusion, but by his lack of self-control when Mommy tells him what to do. "Solomon would say that this situation is about a five-year-old boy's waywardness. 'Foolishness is bound up in the heart of a child; the rod of discipline will remove it far from him' [22:15]. He's simple, and he has to be trained. And if she trains him in self-control, he will become more confident. For instance, Solomon says that a man who can control his spirit is better than one who captures a city [16:32]. I notice that when I train my boys to control themselves, their self-confidence increases. When they realize that they *can* redirect their emotions, and when they know *how*, they're more secure when they interact."

Our friend's problem, I said, is not her son's gender, but his childish anger. There are two sound reasons for saying so. First, a five-year-old does not have the physical development that drives his sexuality. Second, he doesn't have the psychological development to be self-aware about such an abstract issue as gender.

I concluded, "If we self-indulgently try to reeducate people about the decline of Judeo-Christian culture when they're in agony over their children's problems, we're going to miss opportunities for clear answers that will give them the biblical principles they need when they're most open to hearing them."

With that sermon, I was sure that I had laid an egg. *So let's pray for all those evangelistic opportunities we may get twenty years from now.*

A week later, my friend Larry told me a humbling story. When he arrived home after hearing my sermon, a local friend of his called with the exact problem I had outlined. Larry was able to use the approach I had suggested that morning to redirect the conversation. Larry's friend left the conversation encouraged because he learned that his desires for his child's self-esteem were attainable, and that the Bible shows a well-constructed road. He also learned that, in his fears for his child, he was not backward, bigoted, or crazy.

I'm not saying that this is *the* answer for parents of transgender toddlers. These kinds of issues are often too complex for simple solutions. I'm not saying that this alone will win such people to Christ. I am saying that in order to win those trying to make a bankrupt philosophy of life work, I have to have compassion. I have to realize that I'm not answering questions so much as I'm answering people.

BECOMING A HEALER: LISTENING

For one day, observe the way you answer people. After each conversation, no matter what the topic is, note the following details:

- What were the key words that initiated your replies?
- Looking back, did you respond to the right key words, or was the person actually emphasizing other words?
- How might you have determined what the right key words were?

11

CONFRONT A FRIEND

On February 20, 2007, an article shot to the top of the *New York Times* most e-mailed list. Daniel Goleman's piece was called, "Flame First, Think Later: New Clues to E-Mail Misbehavior."[1] It explored what causes a person to send rude messages. A significant part of this essay's message came from the section of the *Times* in which it was published. It was categorized under "Health."

Fifty years ago, a newspaper article about angry or inappropriate behavior would have been about an incident, not about social patterns. To merit coverage, the incident would have been remarkable—an extremely ill-judged speech at the Rotary luncheon, perhaps, or a criminal act like brawling. The article would have been categorized as "News." No one at that time would have written about the emerging pattern of impulsive letter-composition.

People's inhibitions were such that rude behavior was newsworthy. Descriptions of the bizarre were reserved for salacious novels—if you could find them.

Today, according to Goleman, incidents of rudeness come in "a steady stream of instant messages" like those sent and received by middle-schoolers. The stream is copious enough to be studied in "the emerging field of social neuroscience" and analyzed in Goleman's essay. And because the problem is so common, his essay gets sent hither and yon by impulsive e-mailers. The essay is not "News" because flaming is not unusual. Rather, flaming is such a common affliction that people need information in order to deal with it—as with all the other problems in "Health."

Flaming is "sending a message that is taken as offensive, embarrassing or downright rude." The cause of it, psychologists say, is the "online disinhibition effect." When someone is at the keyboard, his inhibitions are lowered by his "anonymity" online, his "invisibility" to others, "the exaggerated sense of self from being alone," and the absence of an "authority figure." There is also a "time lag between sending an e-mail message and getting feedback."

Goleman elucidates the science of that time lag.

When two people interact directly, they send a wealth of social information back and forth with their facial expressions, tones of voice, and body language. "[T]he brain reads a continual cascade of emotional signs and social cues, instantaneously using them to guide our next move so that the encounter goes well." The person typing at a keyboard receives no such instant feedback, and when he's deprived of it, his words become less and less inhibited.

Goleman cites a 2002 experiment with pairs of college students getting to know each other online from separate booths. "While coming and going into the lab, the students were well behaved. But the experimenter was stunned to see the messages many of the students sent. About 20 percent of the e-mail conversations immediately became outrageously lewd or simply rude."

Lower the inhibitions and self-expression takes a nasty turn.

Flaming is only one example of the rudeness that now plagues our culture. We endure emotional violence on the road, in line at the store, from the indifference of bureaucracies, and from unethical corporations. We have to steel ourselves against a relentless assault on our sense of well-being—an assault that our society can only seem to explain as a matter of public health.

This social condition offers evangelicals an opportunity. Something as simple as flaming provides a window into the depths of the human soul, a window people will look through if evangelicals can master Jesus' way of confrontation.

Confrontation: The act of making an implicit conflict explicit.

No doubt many readers wish that confrontation had been the first issue we explored in this book. Many evangelicals are angry at the state of American culture and want to find more effective arguments, punchier punch lines, distinctions that are blacker and whiter. They would say that evangelicals need to do more confronting, that evangelicals have not been bold enough in delineating right and wrong. For them the approach of this book is too equivocal and soft.

But there is a reason why we take up confrontation last.

The Psalm at Sychar's Gate

John pushed through a throng of Sychar's finest, none of whom would make way for him.[2] He felt no remorse knocking shoulders with a white-robed Samaritan priest. The priest looked John up and down with the wrinkles on his forehead contorted and finally turned his back.

Free of the crowd, John looked at the bread he had bought and cursed the extortionate baker, who wouldn't even acknowledge John's presence until all the Samaritans had been served and who refused to budge on his price. John glanced around the marketplace looking for the rest of the disciples. He finally spotted them huddled in the shade of an olive tree and watching the townsfolk out of the corners of their eyes.

As John approached, he saw Judas Iscariot scowl at him. Judas's voice was tight. "What took you so long?"

John nodded back at the market. "Samaritan greed."

Peter was already trudging back toward Sychar's gate, bellowing, "Let's get out of here!" loud enough for some Samaritan women to benefit from his scorn.

As they passed by the city elders in the gate, John heard his brother James chanting, "Great is the Lord, and greatly to be praised, in the city of our God, His holy mountain." One of the Samaritan elders spat. James shot a cock-eyed grin at John.

Finally the twelve men were in the open country, making speed back to the well where they had left Jesus. James looked at the peak of Mt. Gerizim, and then back at Sychar. "They could use some of the Lord's thunder and lightning around here. Might purge their heresies."

John gave up a mirthless laugh. "Not enough. How about a little fire from heaven like Elijah used to call? Between their idolatry under the Greeks and their abominations in the temple under Herod, these half-breeds have exhausted the Lord's patience."

When the twelve rounded the bend and saw the well, John felt a stab in his gut and stopped in the middle of the road. Jesus was talking with the woman they had passed on their way into the city. She was leaning toward Jesus, as if she could drink from his words, her face round with a kind of fear. All at once, she bolted from Jesus and ran past John and the others like a rabbit. Her water pot stood on the edge of the well, forsaken.

John looked at James, who evaded John's eyes. There was a tense silence among the twelve. Without a word, they set out some food, while Jesus seemed to watch the woman's trail of dust. John tore a piece of bread and held it out to Jesus. "Rabbi, eat." The others watched.

The rabbi's face seemed to pursue the disciples' eyes, but caught none, and finally turned to John. John lifted the bread closer, and Jesus stared at it without comment. At length he bounced up from where he sat on the well, looked again down the road, and rubbed his hands. "I have food you know nothing about. My food is to do the will of him who sent me and to accomplish his work. It was necessary for me to go through Samaria. It was the decree of my Father. We have a harvest to bring in among these people, and all the nourishment I need is to finish that harvest. I sent you to reap too."

Confrontation at Sychar's Well

The disciples were called to heal relationships in Samaria using Jesus as a model, called to reap souls for eternal life. One tool they needed in winning those souls was confrontation. They needed to expose Samaritan errors and sins. But, at this point, the disciples did not have the same method of confrontation as Jesus.

Confrontation, in Jesus' method with the Samaritan woman, was a useful tool only after he had created a strong relationship. Jesus crossed the barriers that kept the woman from him. He evaded the woman's boxes, conversing with her relationally rather than ideologically. He worked with her to process the crucible experiences of her life. When she asked questions, he answered them directly. In this context Jesus' confrontations, far from weakening the woman's relationship with him, actually strengthened it.

Consider the woman's response after Jesus confronted her divorces and immorality (4:29). She left her pot and ran back to the men of Sychar—likely some of the very ones who had participated in her humiliations and sins—and announced, "Come, see a man who told me all the things that I have done." She viewed Jesus' pinpointing of her sins as a healing experience, something that others should want to see for themselves. She felt that they would desire the same peace and clarity in their own consciences. She did not feel thrashed by Jesus, or she never would have advertised his powers of confrontation.

Also consider how she responded when Jesus confronted her ignorance. We have already seen the stark nature of his statement (4:22): "You [Samaritans] worship what you do not know; we worship what we know, for salvation is from the Jews." He was saying that the Samaritan Pentateuch was inadequate to instruct them about Yahweh and his plans and that the knowledge of living water came only from the Jewish Scriptures.

If Jesus had not built a strong relational context with the woman, this statement would have been inflammatory, would have shut down the dialogue entirely. But Jesus *had* built that relational context. She received his statement not as point-scoring, but as teaching. The idea that God was her Father and that she could worship him in a community beyond Gerizim and Jerusalem was pure hope. Because she trusted Jesus, his confrontation of her culture's ignorance was another step toward life.

When Jesus taught his disciples about reaping the harvest of souls (John 4:34–38), he was saying that they were called to join him in this kind of healing confrontation. The self-indulgent confrontations they had made before—perhaps chanting Psalm 48 through Sychar's gate—would have no place in this work. To reap the fruit Jesus had sown, they would have to deal with people his way.

A Tool for Healing

I suspect the reason most evangelicals hesitate to confront people of the diversity culture is not cowardice. Neither is the reason a sense of jealousy over social status or anger over American culture's degradation, or lack of confidence in their own convictions. I suspect the reason is that they don't want to make unfounded accusations.

Most evangelicals sense that the people around them have experienced the toxic mixture of being sinned against and committing sin. Evangelicals are not deaf to the stories of abuse that come out of every institution in our society, from the family to the school to the church. They feel their obligation not to lob accusations at the victims of sin. But they also know that every person is a sinner. Many are tired of preaching that skirts the issue of disobedience against God. So they wonder how to confront others with the reality of sin without being unjust.

Accusation: A charge against a person that is either just or unjust.

I believe there is a clear path out of this dilemma.

In my experience, a healing confrontation does not involve accusation. A Christlike confronter does not make charges about a person's motivations and then lay out evidence to prove his case. For instance, Jesus did not say to the Samaritan woman, "You are consumed with lust, and that's why you've lost five husbands and now live in disgrace."

Rather, in my experience, a healing confrontation involves two steps. First, someone points to my specific behaviors that are wrong. He names these behaviors without comment. Jesus named observable facts about the woman's past—five husbands, one boyfriend—giving no recorded judgment about why her life had gone so badly. Second, the person defines choices about how I can change, laying out various paths I can take in dealing with my sin. Jesus defined the Samaritan woman's choices in terms of worship: if she wanted to gain living water, she needed to worship the Father in spirit and truth.

I now practice confrontation without accusation for two reasons.

To begin with, I can't take the true measure of a person's sins until I know her motivations. Jesus knew when to level an accusation and when to be gentle because he was given knowledge of people's thoughts. Take John 8, where Jesus confronts both gently and harshly. To the woman caught in adultery, Jesus is gentle (8:2–11). When he hears that none of her accusers has condemned her, he says, "I do not condemn you, either. Go. From now on sin no more." But later, to "those Jews who had believed Him," Jesus is scathing (8:31–38). "You seek to kill Me, because My word has no place in you." The difference between the affirming exhortation and the thunderous smackdown is in the motivations Jesus perceives in the two audiences.

Furthermore, for an accusation to be just, it must be specific: it must say precisely what a person did wrong and why. Since I cannot read people's hearts and cannot know precisely what motivates their sinful behaviors, I don't know enough to level a specific accusation. People trespass God's law because of a mixture of selfishness, doctrinal error, and ignorance. If I cannot untangle that mixture with certainty—and I can't—then I must not make accusations. I believe this is not a matter of tact in my speech, but a matter of justice in my speech.

Simply put, I don't know enough to accuse justly. All I know is what I see.

Opportunities for Healing

As we've observed, flaming is only one kind of abusive behavior that people face daily. I regularly hear friends describe to me how they pressure their spouses, children, and coworkers with accusations and outbursts. My friends usually think they're winning me to their side with this slashing approach, when they're actually telling me why their conflicts arose in the first place. They present me with opportunities to show them a window into their souls.

To show this window, I use three different kinds of confrontation, which I present here from the subtlest to the most blunt.

1. *Give a new point of view.*

My friend Carlos and I first met at a lecture, and our brief conversation seemed to promise a thriving friendship. I knew very few people who had similar interests to mine, so when he asked if we could talk more, I eagerly agreed. But in our ensuing conversations each week, Carlos's anger began to emerge. He was angry at his parents, at his many ex-friends, at professors from the university where he had just gotten his degree.

Somehow Carlos needed to get a view of his soul, and he was asking for my input.

I could have used his openness as a pretext to say, "Carlos, you're living for yourself. The reason you've broken all these relationships is your self-focus." But I wanted our friendship to grow. I felt that even though Carlos was opening up to me, he had not asked for an assessment of his life that was so stark. I felt I still needed to earn his trust. Furthermore, I wasn't sure precisely *how* he was living for himself. In his anger, was Carlos malicious toward others, or was he merely unwise? Had he ever been taught that there were ways to resolve anger—taught in a way that he could understand? Malice might warrant a blunt statement, but ignorance would not.

I took a risk. I introduced Carlos to the new perpective that all life was designed to glorify God by asking him to read Romans 1. What did that passage say was the one cause of all the world's problems? I was deeply afraid that exposing this well-educated man to that chapter would torpedo our friendship. But by the next week, he had embraced the point: our refusal to glorify God is the reason we do wrong. Carlos began to apply the principle, week by week, to his relationships with friends, with his parents, even to his finances.

This new point of view gave him the soul-window he needed.

Months later, he reviewed the process of repeatedly choosing humility over anger and the blessings he had received by exercising faith in Jesus' promises. "Shouldn't I call myself a Christian?"

Presenting a new point of view gives a friend another take on his anger without commenting on him personally. I use this approach when my friend is relatively new and when I want to give him freedom to respond any way he feels is right. I get the best results when I present the new perspective as a model that applies to me, revealing something about myself rather than making an accusation.

2. Decline to agree with excuses.

One day my friend Greg was listing all the reasons why he had a right to be angry with his coworkers.

I had talked with Greg often on his breaks at the restaurant where he worked, usually about books, music, or news. We sometimes rambled into philosophy.

But on this day he'd had enough of his coworkers' attitudes. Listing the examples by pulling back the fingers on his left hand, he told me that the other employees were giving him dirty looks, that they stopped their conversations whenever he walked by, and that they made one sarcastic comment to him after another. Then he described how he met these offenses look for look, silence for silence, comment for comment, eye for eye, tooth for tooth—laughing bitterly at the need for him to be so clever.

"I am done with them. I am done." Greg waved his hands like he was parting thick curtains, and sat back.

I have what I call my "don't-know-about-that" face. It consists of a slight pull at the side of my mouth, a quick cocking of my chin in the opposite direction, a squint in my right eye, a squeeze of my eyebrows, together with the suggestion of a shrug. It's a useful face to make, because it doesn't go so far as to say, "Dude, you're lame," but it does communicate that the sale hasn't yet closed and that the route to *sold* is uphill.

When Greg sat back to take a fresh breath, I made this face. Then I pulled my mug over and took a sip of coffee. And I said nothing.

Greg sighed. "Maybe it doesn't have anything to do with me. Maybe I'm overreacting." The backpedaling had begun.

My unwillingness to affirm his excuses gave him a clear enough view of his soul that he turned around.

This is a more direct confrontation than the first. But it still gives a friend some freedom in responding. He can change the subject. He can concede a point or two, or he can do an about-face, as Greg did. If the friend is open, the conversation can lead straight to the gospel.

3. *Define options.*

Trevor had just broken up with his girlfriend. Or rather, she broke up with him *after* he had broken up with her—meaning it was indeed The End. He was slumped over an Americano.

I had spent a fair amount of time with Trevor, and we had talked about many quite personal things. So he was giving me the blow-by-blow of the last day, and I listened even though I dreaded what was coming. I knew him well enough to anticipate how he had handled the argument, and I knew that I had to give him a straight shot of truth—the one thing I didn't want to do.

And the moment came. In their final argument, he said, he had demanded that she answer whether she truly loved him while hooked up to a polygraph. He had told her right where she could go for the test. Name, address, phone number.

I leaned in. "Trevor, you can't talk to someone that way."

There were several things I did not say to him. I didn't label him an abusive man just because at that moment he fit some abstract profile. I didn't say what others had told him, that he had chemical imbalances in his brain—that in other words he was mentally ill and needed to "get help." I didn't characterize his motivations religiously, either, giving him verses about how the heart is deceitful above all else. All of those statements would have been accusations.

I stuck to his behavior, as he had described it on his own. I said, "You can't do that." *Why* he had done it was beyond my power to know.

He looked at one of the floor tiles. It wasn't necessary for me to explain myself, because he knew what he had done and was beyond trying to justify it.

My interjection at that point was not the end of the confrontation. Merely saying what he already knew was not presenting the full truth to him. The full truth included how he should live now that their relationship had ended. The full truth included options.

I talked with him about the option of carrying his bad experiences into the next relationship, defining someone else according to his previous experiences. He already wanted to avoid that route. I told him that he could treat this as a health issue, that some people would recommend drugs he could take for anxiety. He wasn't convinced of that one either. So I told him about the only other option that I saw, which was for his soul to be wiped clean from those experiences by the resurrected Jesus.

He listened. The options made a window on his inner life—without my telling him what I thought was down there.

This level of confrontation is direct and personal. With some relationships, I get to this level in an hour. With others, it takes years. But I am always pursuing it, because it avoids labeling someone with accusations, while at the same time it defines choices for a soul in process.

At the contested wells of our society, confrontation is not optional. Unless we deal with the nature of sin—deal with it specifically and unsparingly—we are not faithful in presenting the gospel. But confrontation does not have to leave others feeling demeaned. It should be for us what it was for Jesus—a powerful tool of healing.

BECOMING A HEALER: JUSTICE

- Before your next confrontation, write down all the accusations in your mind against the other person.
- Conduct the confrontation any way you see fit.
- After the confrontation, review your list of accusations and check how many of them were just.
- Evaluate your conduct during the confrontation to see whether your accusations helped or hindered a resolution.

12

IMAGINE THE SCENE

The Baptist's suit looked even worse up close. The dark blue was flat, probably dyed by child laborers somewhere in India to keep it cheap. The jacket button pulled against enormous pressure from his stomach, and the folds and creases seemed to protest that the jacket had never seen the dry cleaners.

The woman could see the title of the Chuck Colson book as she sat down next to the Baptist—*God and Government*. "From thug to theocrat," she thought. The pages were dog-eared and underlined with arrows and comments scrawled in the margins, and the Baptist had tagged his favorite parts with little exclamation points. Was this the fourth time he'd read it?

She pulled out her copy of *Mother Jones*, and slapped it on the table with the cover up. George W. Bush was drawn like the wicked witch from *The Wizard of Oz*, green and about to be melted, and the cover's headline read, "25 Ways To Lift the Curse."[1] She dawdled, taking a long sip of her mocha, so that the Baptist got a chance to see how much she loved the evangelical president. Then she turned to the article she had wanted to read about the initiatives to ban gay marriage in several states: "Will Gay Marriage Help McCain?"[2]

She felt the Baptist's eyes on *Mother Jones*. In her peripheral vision, she could see his multiple chins turn toward her, and then drop back to his book. After the third time, she shifted in her seat.

"Can I ask what you're reading?"

The voice had gravel in it, but it wasn't from Mississippi. It sounded to her like the Baptist was from New York, or somewhere in the northeast. Born and bred. She stared at his face, trying to find a clue about his background. He looked to her like a mechanic.

He wore an expression that matched his voice's bluntness, and met her eyes without so much as a twitch. "I shouldn't bother you."

"No, no, not at all." She pulled out a smile to pacify his gaze, but felt as if she were blinking ten times a second. The other people at the table were safely focused on their own conversations, so she turned toward him slightly and adopted her patient voice. "I'm reading about gay marriage bans that are being voted on around the country."

"And the presidential election?"

"Exactly."

He smiled and grunted a laugh. "Those initiatives didn't do Kerry much good last time. I happened to be in Ohio before that election, and the ban there definitely got some people to the polls."

She tried to keep her voice from signaling too much interest. "Do you live in Ohio?"

"Nah. I was just there on business."

"Where did you grow up?"

"Belmar, New Jersey, near Trenton. I work for Hartford."

"The insurance company?"

"Yeah. Seemed to offer the best opportunities years ago. Worked my way up. We'll see if there are any opportunities left when this financial mess is over."

"For sure. Are you here on business now?"

"I live here. Up near Sacramento. They moved me to the West Coast ten years ago. I'm just killing time before I pick up some people at the airport today."

"Meeting family?"

"Kind of a long story. A couple years ago, my wife and I hosted a Japanese student for a month. There's an organization that brings English students over here as a cultural exchange. Afterward, she kept writing to us and we kept writing to her—e-mail and all that. We kind of bonded, I guess you might say. So she's coming back with her parents."

"What a great story!"

"Yeah. I've always been fascinated by Japanese culture. By the formality, I guess. I wanted to dress right for her parents, but I haven't bought a suit since I moved. All they know is sport coats out here, so this old thing will have to do." He pulled his mouth sidelong and shrugged. "Anyways, this girl is pretty special to us." He looked away, then back. "I assume you live here."

The woman nodded. "East bay. I have a graphic design studio around the corner." She saw him glance at her portfolio. "But I grew up in the valley. Dad says I moved to the Gay Area—and he's not really teasing."

The Baptist grunted again. "Conservative?"

"*Oh* yeah." She looked at the Baptist's book. "Dad and I don't get along real well."

His cool eyes scanned the café while he took another sip. "You take your politics pretty seriously."

She looked away. "It's not just politics between Dad and me. He thinks I'm going to hell."

His eyes shot back to her. "So you grew up in church."

She nodded.

"What brand?"

She smiled and sat up straight. "First Baptist of the Valley."

"Baptist, huh. That explains your old man. And maybe why you're here."

"I just had to get out." She smiled. "I kind of took you for a Baptist, actually."

Now he really laughed, the gravel grinding away in his throat and his lungs betraying his smoker's wheeze. "Lady, I was born Irish Catholic. They wrapped me in a green blanket and spiked my bottle with whiskey."

She grinned and shook her head. "I guess I need to get out more."

"You sure do."

"But I see you're into the born again hatchet man." She pointed to his book.

"Colson?" He looked at the cover and pulled his mouth again. "Okay, you've got an excuse. Evangelical Republican. Opposes gay marriage." They chuckled. "Yeah, I have come to appreciate Colson. I like a lot of his points. He writes as if Christians should have brains."

"So would you consider yourself an evangelical?"

"Yeah. That is, I would now." He leaned over a bit. "I'm Johnny-come-lately to them. In a lot of ways, I don't fit the church I'm attending. Don't get some of the attitudes. These kids get up there and whine and they really believe they're singing. The preacher is okay, but I guess there isn't a lot there for me."

"What do you mean? If the church doesn't speak to you, why do you go?"

He stared at her evenly for a moment, and then looked away. "Because, there's more to life than having everything just how I like. Had to learn it the hard way."

"Sounds like you've got quite a story. How does an insurance executive learn that?"

"By getting cancer, watching his hair go white in his forties, and not being able to talk to his wife about life and death because she hates the sound of his voice." He looked back at her. "Got me thinking, reading."

"So you're a survivor. Did you remarry?"

His eyebrows shot up. "What makes you think my wife split?"

More blinking, but she regained her calm when she saw his smile. "I guess that's how it usually goes when a woman hates the sound of a man's voice."

"Yeah, usually. And, lady, if she had split, I would've deserved it. But she and I learned an interesting word—forgiveness. You grew up in church. You know all about that. But I had to come to it as an adult, with a load of baggage."

"Well, it's commendable that you and your wife are still together."

"It's not commendable. It was an act of God." He took another sip of coffee. "Anyways, seeing my life change the way I did puts things in perspective. I try to set the irritating stuff at my church aside. They know the same Jesus I know."

"Jesus is real to you."

"Yeah." He paused before taking another sip. "That's pretty existential, but yeah. He's real to me. He became real to our Japanese girl too. That's why she's bringing her parents here." He scanned the café again. "So what's the deal with you and your old man? If you don't mind my asking."

The woman took a deep breath.

Conclusion

BELONGING AT CAFÉ SIDDHARTHA

I don't fit anywhere. Never have. And I'm not complaining.

I can function well in secular universities, for example, but my biblically focused faith makes me stick out. I can also function well in my small-town church, but my devotion to classical music is something few in the congregation share. There doesn't seem to be a group of people that shares my exact priorities.

Family dysfunction is not what made me this way. Most of my relatives have enjoyed long marriages. My brother and I were brought up to know Jesus Christ. We received abundant love from our parents and grandparents, and their vehicle for this love was abundant time—training us, laughing with us (and at us), and conversing with us. As a result, I feel that I carry home around with me, regardless of how out of place I might be.

But my family is a strange confluence of cultural streams. Here are some of them.

On my mother's side, I am descended from Danish immigrants. My great-grandfather came to America in his teens and hopped a train to Nebraska, where he became a dairyman.

My Grandpa Ted and Grandma Shirley grew up speaking Danish, persevered as children through the Depression, and had their own dairy for a time. Grandpa was the Sunday school director at the Lutheran church in Council Bluffs, Iowa. But he and Grandma got saved at a Billy Graham crusade, and the church never accepted their new faith. So they sold their land and drove to California with their three children in the winter of 1954. Grandpa wore out more sets of chains in that one trip over the Rockies than I will ever use in my life. He became a contractor, and the family helped start a new church in Chico—a church where they still take part and where their son-in-law, my dad, is now on staff.

Grandma inherited all the skills and interests of those who fought to preserve their way of life against the cataclysms of the 1930s and 1940s. She sewed and did needlepoint. She canned and cleaned. She made food a vehicle for joy. She still has the most prodigious memory for names and connections I have ever known. More than once, I've watched her sit down with total strangers in towns far from home and, in a methodical interviewing style, discover people they knew in common.

Grandpa loves wood. He is a maker. He carved the wooden spoon that hangs in Grandma's kitchen. He made toy trucks, guns, and puzzles. He took junk and refashioned it into furniture.

But one day when I was a boy, Grandpa did something new. He emerged from his workshop with a swan. It was life-sized, made from blocks of hardwood that were glued together with such skill that they appeared seamless. The swan he had carved and sanded out of this wood was intuitively proportioned, her neck rising with an unselfconscious elegance. She was abstract, a composition devoted to shape. Aside from the two amber beads discretely inset as eyes, Grandpa made no other surface effects such as etching feathers onto her folded wings. Yet, cool as she was, she looked like she would burst at the slightest noise out of the pond in which she swam.

From where did the swan emerge? How did Grandpa leap from craft to sculpture? Why? I still don't know.

His daughter, my mom, has an eye for color and an ear for literature. She read to me from my infancy in a voice that became small with pleasure. She speaks with an understanding of words, with selected emphasis, and yet without affectation of any kind. She always has a book going, usually something to do with history. Her appreciation of words is second only to her visual sensitivity. She has a natural talent for interior design, making colors not just match but dialogue. Our homes always glowed with conversing hues.

Again, why? Where did her interest in books come from? Where could her sense of design have been nourished? Her childhood memories are of grinding poverty. I think she knew hunger. Her parents were people of physical labor. There wasn't time or energy for aesthetics.

On my dad's side, my great-grandfathers were very different from each other. One was a cowboy—the real deal. Popo, as my dad called him, was short, but he could wrestle. He had a technique for pinning very large men faster than you could shout, "Yippee ki-yay." He used it at church picnics. The other was T.J., the mayor of his southern California town, and a kind of local aristocrat. In an old photograph, he appraises you from behind round, wire spectacles—a man not easily fooled. Yet he made dresses for his two daughters, and loved to cook.

T.J.'s daughter Mae was of the town, not the land. She was a bohemian free-spirit who played the violin. For most of her adult life she painted, both on canvas and, more exotically, on bone china. This was the full extent of her domestic skills. Her cooking pleased small boys well enough, but no one else. Her standards of hygiene also pleased small boys: why bathe when you have a swimming pool? Grandma's health remedies were tea and soda crackers, which, given the alternatives, small boys again approved. Her passions were wide landscapes, *legato* melodies, and laughter.

The cowboy's son, my Grandpa Vere, was hard to figure. He was every inch a rancher. He broke his own horse and well into his seventies rode a feisty Tennessee Walker named Bomber. For much of his life he had lemon and orange groves, and the last of these ranches, with a many-pillared white house on a hill in Santa Barbara, was the family's template for heaven.

But this rancher had a voice.

In college he started singing baritone roles in opera. He attracted the attention of two top voice coaches in southern California, one of them a specialist in *lieder*, the genre of German art song. He would get off his tractor, put on a suit, and go perform in the city. He would vocalize while driving around in his truck, unaware that he was entertaining the whole district until he stepped into a roadside café and the waitress said, "Oh, you're the singer!" He hung around the Claremont Colleges, knew Marilyn Horne, and even sang *lieder* at the Hollywood Bowl.

Again, where did the music come from? How did a cowboy's son, no doubt with little encouragement, emerge in adulthood singing art songs in German?

Then there's Grandpa Vere's son, my dad. A surfer, then a hippy. A hippy who supported the war. Dad is a guitar-player, folk-singer, song-writer, whose fondest memories of college were of studying the twelve-tone compositional system of Arnold Schoenberg. Beyond that, Dad draws, and has a voice as a draftsman that I can see instantly, just as I can hear his voice in the melodies he writes. And he combines all this with a creative, hard-nosed business acumen that embraces risk, builds systems, retains the best workers, and solves problems.

So I don't fit anywhere. The streams that converged to make me who I am are too diverse.

I grew up unafraid of the art world because my family lived in that world. I grew up unafraid of hard work because my family was all about hard work. I grew up bohemian and bourgeois. I am literary among people who don't read, classical among people who've never heard a violin live, conservative among liberals, practical among the intellectual, intellectual among the practical, straight-laced among the immoral, worldly among evangelicals. I reject being put in a box—not because I don't know who I am, but because I do. I reject other people's categories because they are alien, because all the characteristics they regard as contradictions I regard as normal.

I didn't invent this identity. I inherited it.

One day, my parents drove me up to Salem, Oregon, to start life at college. The town of Ashland is the halfway point from our home in Chico, so we stopped for lunch. Ashland is famous for its Shakespearean festival. It's a diversity culture haven, with bookstores, coffee houses, art galleries, and neo-pagan knickknacks. We came to a well belonging to this culture, and we sat down. It was less Café Siddhartha than Café Gaia, the people heavier and frumpier, with older Outbacks rusted from the rain. The diversity culture thrives as much in these small hill towns as in urban centers like San Francisco.

Dad took in the cultural clutter of the place. He looked at the readers slouching over their coffee, examined the art on the brick walls, overheard the key words from conversations in the surrounding booths, and then looked at me for a while. My childhood and adolescent struggle with not fitting anywhere was done. I had managed to leave high school at peace with my peers, having earned acceptance without paying the price of conformity. Dad finally said, "You fit here."

He didn't mean that everything in me was mirrored by the people in that café. He saw that I fit because there was freedom not to fit, that I could grow and breathe in that clutter of interactions. He was saying, *Take the faith that we passed to you, the knowledge of the Scriptures that we encouraged in you, the risen Lord with whom we walk, and live among these people. You were made to leave an impression on these hardened souls.*

I do not believe my experience is unusual. America is full of believers who don't fit anywhere, but who were made to leave an impression.

If you follow Christ, you have a wealth of insight that is uniquely yours.

God has selected pieces of knowledge from far off times and places and has brought the pieces to you. He has selected wise people to carry some of the pieces of knowledge. But to carry other pieces he has selected infuriating and sinful people. God's porters of knowledge, whether wise or sinful, usually did not know what they were carrying, but the sovereign God overruled their conscious intentions, even their good ones, and used the pieces of knowledge they carried to endow you with wealth.

God has also selected experiences for you, many of them agonizing—experiences that make you feel cut off from others. You have suffered losses that the people around you cannot value, betrayals that sting you alone, and punishing struggles for competence that others cannot appreciate. You also have moments of breakthrough that leave others cold because they cannot see the significance. You have felt high satisfaction from completing work that only a small coterie is able to discern. These experiences, in spite of the isolation they create, are more of the wealth with which God has endowed you.

Your endowments in Christ can often leave you lonely. It is hard to find connections with others in the knowledge and experience you value most deeply. Believers may seem indifferent or even judgmental. And for unbelievers, what Christ has given you may seem too volatile.

This book is a challenge to invest the wealth you've inherited in the souls of believers and unbelievers both. To do this, you may have to overcome a need to fit in. You may have to accept that God's will for your life is to stick out.

Other believers need you to stick out. I think one of the most significant reasons why believers have not won more souls for Christ is an overdose of conformity. The average evangelical has become a small person, attending churches full of people just like her, rarely venturing out of the bubble of evangelical entertainment, hearing other perspectives only in a posture of defensiveness. You and your endowments are needed in the Father's household. The believers around you can become larger people if you invest your wealth in them.

But this book shows that unbelievers also need the endowments Christ has given you. As long as they think of Christian spirituality in terms of the group they know as evangelicals, they will not follow Christ. But if you show them the power of the risen Jesus in your testimony, the freedom you have found through the Scriptures, and the love you have stirred in members of Christ's family—stirred with the nonconformity I recommended back in chapter 6—I think unbelievers will see the gospel for the first time. I think, in fact, that you can only show the gospel to the people of the diversity culture as an individual. You have to stick out.

True, lots of people stick out in ways that are merely provocative. Like I did.

At college, as I described in the introduction, I found that my individuality did not give me the right kind of credibility to testify about Christ effectively. My strange mixture of traits was intriguing to diversity culture people, I suppose, but it did not make my point of view any more palatable to them. They forgave me for believing the Bible, for talking about Christ, for going into the ministry. They forgave me because of my artistic side. But they weren't going to ask for living water just because I played the violin. They probably hoped I'd grow out of my Christianity as they'd watched so many others do before.

As I discovered, the thing that kept me from winning souls was my self-indulgence. I was too confident that I knew the people I was dealing with, too quick to judge their attitudes and experiences.

My gospel was self-indulgent too. It consisted of the points I wanted to make rather than the truths people needed to hear. I wanted to say that there were moral absolutes, and I wanted to pile up the evidence. I wanted to prove the inerrancy of Scripture. I wanted to expound the doctrines of total depravity and election. All of the things I wanted to say are true. But most of my peers were trying to figure out if their parents loved them. They needed the truth of the gospel applied to them specifically. (Abstract coherence is one of the most insidious forms of self-indulgence I have. It allows me to ignore the hot problems around me in favor of cool formulas.)

But God is faithful. Over time, faster than I deserved, he taught me that, while my individuality set me up to win people from the diversity culture, my self-indulgence set me up to fail. I stuck out in ways that destroyed my credibility.

I hope this book has shown that Jesus stuck out in ways that gave healing. He understood the woman at the well from God's story, not Israel's, and he was rigorous in distinguishing the two. I also hope the book has communicated some of what God showed me as I tried to repent of my self-indulgence. I hope it has shown that our repentance from ungodliness enhances our individuality, and can be the most powerful tool God uses to win others to himself.

John says that when Jesus departed from Judea for Galilee, it was necessary for him to go through Samaria (4:4). Geographically speaking, it was not necessary. Jews from Judea traveled around Samaria, in the same way and for the same reasons that evangelicals have routes around the diversity culture. The interactions were distasteful.

So why was Jesus' Samaritan route *necessary?* The answer lies in John's use of the Greek word. He only uses it nine other times in his gospel, and five of those uses are in the immediate context of chapters three and four (3:7, 14, 30; 4:20, 24; 9:4; 10:16; 12:34; 20:9). In each of these nine instances, the word refers to something divinely ordained or commanded—as in, "You *must* be born again" and "He *must* rise again from the dead" (3:7; 20:9; emphasis added). It was necessary for Jesus to travel that Samaritan road because the Father sought the Samaritan woman. Jesus was under a compulsion from his Father to sit at the contested well and heal her. The Father's story about her was that she was a future worshiper.

I believe it is necessary for us to win souls at Café Siddhartha.

I believe that God's will is for a woman in her Outback to switch off the discussion of bigotry on the radio, flee with her leather portfolio into the Tibetan aura of Café Siddhartha, take her mocha and smile at the laughing Buddha, and spy the only available chair at a common table. The chair that sits right beside you.

NOTES

Introduction: The Chair in Café Siddhartha

1. USAToday/Gallup, October 10–12, 2008, http://www.usatoday.com/news/politics/election2008/poll-tracker.htm.

2. *San Francisco Chronicle*, Monday, October 13, 2008, http://www.sfgate.com.

3. Perry Garfinkle, "In Buddha's Path On the Streets of San Francisco," *New York Times*, October 10, 2008, http://travel.nytimes.com/.

4. David Brooks, "The Class War Before Palin," *New York Times*, October 10, 2008, http://www.nytimes.com/.

5. "The 'Last Lynching': How Far Have We Come?" *Talk of the Nation*, NPR, October 13, 2008, http://www.npr.org/templates/story/story.php?storyId=95672737.

6. The definition of the term *evangelical* is much debated. To construct a theological definition is an important task, but beyond the scope of this book. I am using the term to refer to members of the subculture I describe. The focus of this book is on the relationship between the culture of evangelicals with American consumer society and with the culture represented by Café Siddhartha.

7. "The Samaritans believed that Joshua built a sanctuary on Mt. Gerizim, which was the center for all early Israelite worship." *The Zondervan Pictorial Encyclopedia of the Bible*, ed. Merrill C. Tenney (Grand Rapids: Zondervan, 1975), s.v. "Samaritans."

8. "There is no exact date for this event. Josephus (Jos. Antiq. XI. viii. 1–4) tells of the building of this temple, but the account is so confused that different scholars, on the basis of the evidence, date the building of this temple anywhere from the time of Nehemiah to the time of Alexander the Great." Ibid.

9. The Samaritan Pentateuch substituted "Mt. Gerizim for Mt. Ebal as the

place where the law was to be written on the stones of the altar (Deut 27:4)." Ibid., s.v. "Samaritan Pentateuch, The."

10. "Samaria was finally captured and destroyed by Hyrcanus (as evidenced in archaeological excavations) and its citizens exiled. . . . Thus, the way to Galilee was opened to the Jews." Yohanan Aharoni and Michael Avi-Yonah, *The Macmillan Bible Atlas*, rev. ed. (New York: Macmillan, 1977), 131.

11. Jesus traveled north from Judea with his disciples. He would have reached Jacob's well, which is south of Sychar, before reaching the city. His disciples left him at the well and continued north while the Samaritan woman journeyed south on the same road. She likely passed them at some point (see John 4:3–6, 8).

12. This incident is fictional, yet I offer it as the kind of insult the disciples might have made. Their attitudes toward Samaritans remained bigoted long after seeing Jesus in conversation with the woman (e.g., Luke 9:51–56).

Chapter 1: Stories from New York, Frisco, and Sychar

1. MRI NYT Reader Profile, http://www.nytimes.whsites.net/mediakit/pdfs/newspaper/MRI_NYTreaderprofile.pdf.

2. Ralph Blumenthal, "Museum Field Trip Deemed Too Revealing," *New York Times*, September 30, 2006, http://www.nytimes.com/.

3. H. W. Janson, *History of Art*, 4th ed., rev. Anthony F. Janson (New York: Henry M. Abrams, 1991), 729.

4. Paul Johnson, *Art: A New History* (New York: HarperCollins, 2003), 668.

5. Flavius Josephus, *The Antiquities of the Jews*, in *The Complete Works of Josephus*, trans. William Whiston, ed. William S. LaSor (Grand Rapids: Kregel, 1981).

6. Ibid., 212.

7. Ibid.

8. Ibid., 232. The biblical account places this incident at the laying of the foundations (Ezra 3:10–13), while Josephus places it "when the temple was finished." Both accounts agree the confused sound of rejoicing and weeping was "heard far away" (Ezra 3:13).

9. Josephus, *Antiquities*, 232.

10. Ibid. Again, the biblical account differs slightly. The opening to Zerubbabel is not directly connected to the sound of rejoicing and weeping. While Josephus implies the opening is a general sentiment of the Samaritan people, the implication of Ezra's account is that the opening comes strictly from "the enemies of Judah and Benjamin" (4:1–3). My interest is not in the accuracy of Josephus's reporting, but

in the fact that such stories were in circulation at the time of Christ, whether accurate or not.

11. Josephus, *Antiquities*, 232.

Chapter 2: Personal Identity on Saturday

1. Susan Dominus, "The Starbucks Aesthetic," *New York Times*, October 22, 2006, http://www.nytimes.com/.

2. Flavius Josephus, *The Antiquities of the Jews*, in *The Complete Works of Josephus*, trans. William Whiston, ed. William S. LaSor (Grand Rapids: Kregel, 1981), 377.

3. "Divorce takes place at the pleasure of the husband, who gives a bill of divorce, according to Dt. 24. . . ." James A. Montgomery, *The Samaritans: The Earliest Jewish Sect* (Philadelphia: J. C. Winston, 1907), 42, http://www.houseofdavid.ca/.

Chapter 3: Street Postmodernism

1. Reprinted with the permission of Simon and Schuster, Inc. from *Bobos in Paradise: The New Upper Class and How They Got There* by David Brooks. Copyright © 2000 by David Brooks. Quotation taken from page 10.

2. Ibid.

3. Ibid., 237.

4. Ibid., 227.

5. Ibid.

6. Ibid., 224–25.

7. Ibid., 224.

8. Ibid., 243.

9. Ibid., 249.

10. Ibid., 247.

11. Ibid., 248–49.

12. Ibid., 249–50.

13. Ibid., 246–47, 250.

14. In making this assertion, I want to be specific about my inference. Certainly, to say the Samaritan woman was an ancient postmodern would be nonsense, and even to imply that what I am calling her street philosophy prefigured postmodernism in some way would be superficial. Rather, I infer from the woman's handling of the conversation that she has a settled mode in which she can relate to someone like Jesus—a Jewish traveler whose attitudes open the possibility of real dialogue. I do not claim that her street philosophy can be fully

reconstructed from this text, nor do I think such a reconstruction is necessary. I present the scene that follows with some touches as to what her thoughts might have been. I do so merely to bring to life the kind of role a street philosophy would have had in this conversation, not to imply that all my suggestions are exegetically derived.

15. Flavius Josephus, *The Antiquities of the Jews*, in *The Complete Works of Josephus*, trans. William Whiston, ed. William S. LaSor (Grand Rapids: Kregel, 1981), 245.

16. Ibid., 377.

17. James A. Montgomery, "The Samaritans in the Talmuds and Other Rabbinic Literature," 167. Montgomery's scholarship is a century old and may at some points be superseded by more recent work, but his book remains standard. I cite him here to show the extent of Jewish-Samaritan interaction.

18. Quoted in ibid., 161.

19. Quoted in ibid., 159.

20. Quoted in ibid., 170.

21. Ibid., 165–95.

22. Ibid., 18–19.

Chapter 4: Truth Out of the Crucible

1. Robin Marantz Henig, "Darwin's God," *New York Times Magazine*, March 4, 2007, http://www.nytimes.com/.

2. Many translators treat John 3:16-21 as a continuing quotation of Jesus' teaching to Nicodemus. In that case, John's record of the dialogue extends to v. 21. My own view is that the dialogue ends in 3:15, and that 3:16–21 is John's comment on Jesus' teaching, which makes the dialogue in chapter 3 slightly shorter than in chapter 4. But these technicalities should not obscure the fact that Jesus' dialogues with Nicodemus and the Samaritan woman are given significant space in the narrative.

3. James A. Montgomery, *The Samaritans: The Earliest Jewish Sect* (Philadelphia: J. C. Winston, 1907), 185, http://www.houseofdavid.ca/.

4. George W. S. Trow, *My Pilgrim's Progress: Media Studies (1950–1998)* (New York: Pantheon, 1999).

5. Ibid., 16.

6. Ibid., 17.

7. Ibid., 18.

Chapter 5: The Power of Scripture

1. Laurie Goodstein, "Evangelicals Fear the Loss of Their Teenagers," *New York Times*, October 6, 2006, http://www.nytimes.com/.

2. I intend the narratives that follow to highlight two features of John's accounts. First, John has bound the scenes of his gospel together tightly, so that each new event propels a story arc. The cleansing of the temple (2:13–22), the dialogue with Nicodemus (3:1–21), and Jesus' calling of witnesses (5:18–47) cannot be interpreted as isolated incidents, but as developments in a deepening conflict that shed light on each other. Specifically, my narratives attempt to show some connections between these incidents. Second, John has focused the reader's attention on the swirl of individual decision-making in the midst of the conflict, encouraging us to draw conclusions about how a character at that time would have interpreted Jesus' actions. John's note about the multitude of followers (2:23–25), his comment about the political aspirations of the crowd (6:14–15), his description of the factions in Jerusalem (7:11–13, 40–44), and his notes about characters' fears (9:22–23; 12:42–43) all show an atmosphere of debate and personal pressure among the rulers and the crowds concerning Jesus. Furthermore, John's selection of individuals like Nicodemus, the Samaritan woman, the blind man (ch. 9), and Martha and Mary (11:17–37; 12:1–8), among others, shows that John views the decision-making as intensely personal. A call for readers to make this decision personally comes in 20:30–31. This context should influence our readings of particular incidents.

3. I intend this narrative to highlight the position the disciples were in when Jesus cleared the temple. The Passover (2:13) drew huge crowds of Jews from many countries, all under the command of the law to sacrifice only at Jerusalem (Deut. 16:2, 5–7). A large proportion of people would have had no choice but to buy a sacrificial animal upon arrival at Jerusalem. Thus, in a space jammed with people and animals, what Jesus did was physically dangerous. It was also as public and high-profile as it could possibly be. The disciples were in the full glare of public attention because of their association with Jesus, and would also have felt the impact of the interrogation Jesus received from the rulers. They had to have a reason for continuing to associate with Jesus after this incident. John says that they found one in Psalm 69, and that the experience became a catalyst for their later faith (John 2:22). I take this as John's application of his own scene to the reader's life.

4. I intend this narrative to highlight Nicodemus's position as a messenger from the Pharisees. It is possible that Nicodemus acted on his own initiative, but

several factors make it unlikely in my view. First, John portrays the Pharisees as a highly cohesive faction that exercised strong internal discipline and succeeded in intimidating outsiders (1:19, 22, 24; 7:45–52; 12:42–43). This portrayal does not encourage us to think of Nicodemus as a lone peacemaker, but as an emissary like those who went to John the Baptist. Second, in my view, Nicodemus delivers a finding from his colleagues to Jesus (3:2). Nicodemus does not profess to give his own personal view, but places himself amongst a group that is agreed: "We know . . ." Third, Jesus is conscious that he is not replying to Nicodemus as an individual, but as a member of a group. He makes the distinction explicit (3:7 characterizing 3:3, 5–6). "Do not be amazed that I said you [singular], 'You [plural] must be born again.'" Jesus' uses of the second person in 3:11–12 are similarly precise: "Truly, truly, I say to you [singular], we speak of what we know . . . and you [plural] do not accept our testimony. If I told you [plural] earthly things and you [plural] do not believe, how will you [plural] believe if I tell you [plural] heavenly things?" Nicodemus is caught between his faction and Jesus' allusion to Numbers 21:1–9, a subplot John works out later (7:50–51; 19:39–40).

5. The logical force of Jesus' argument in John 5:31–47 comes from his reference to two already authenticated legal facts. John the Baptist's testimony had been a matter of official record for some time (1:19–28; 5:33). The signs that Jesus had done were also investigated and affirmed by the rulers (3:2; 5:36). This narrative places a hypothetical but not improbable Pharisee who had been one of John the Baptist's interrogators, and who had also heard Nicodemus's report back to the council from meeting with Jesus, in the audience as Jesus adds the third witness of his Father in the Scriptures. I intend this point of view to highlight the issues such a Pharisee would inevitably have to face, issues to which Jesus explicitly refers (5:44; 12:42–43).

6. James A. Montgomery, *The Samaritans: The Earliest Jewish Sect* (Philadelphia: J. C. Winston, 1907), 286, http://www.houseofdavid.ca/.

7. "The great similarity between the Samaritan Pentateuch and the MT, despite the long period of independent development, argues for the general accuracy of the Torah." *The Zondervan Pictorial Encyclopedia of the Bible*, ed. Merrill C. Tenney (Grand Rapids: Zondervan, 1975).

8. Ibid.

9. Montgomery, *Samaritans*, 287.

10. Ibid., 224–45.

11. I am interpreting the word "spirit" as referring to the doctrine of the new birth, which John has already developed (1:29–34; 3:3–21, 34–36; 4:10, 13–14).

Chapter 6: The Power of Community

1. Patricia Cohen, "Love, Honor, Cherish and Buy," *New York Times*, May 9, 2007, http://www.nytimes.com/.

2. The fact that Jesus is speaking to Jews could be seen as giving encouragement to anti-Semitism. Indeed, the gospel of John has often been accused of feeding anti-Semitic conspiracy theories. But John's presentation of Jesus' teaching is quite specific. The entire world is in darkness, and salvation will not come from inheriting any ethnic heritage (1:3–5, 9–13). Jesus' conflict with the Jewish leaders is centered on their claim to be an exception to the world's darkness and to have no need of a savior from sin (3:3; 5:42–47; 8:31–38). Thus, John's theme is not that the Jews were uniquely wicked, as anti-Semites say, but that they were like everyone else in the world.

3. It is not necessarily clear in 4:23–24 whether John refers to the Holy Spirit or to the general category of spirit as opposed to "flesh" or "blood." I am inclined to think that he refers to the Holy Spirit because of the strong emphasis on the Spirit's role in salvation in the first three chapters of this gospel. The argument against this view would be that John does not use the definite article in 4:23–24, but simply writes "spirit." While the absence of the definite article could be significant, I notice that John does not consistently use it with reference to the Holy Spirit (cf. 1:33, "εν πνευματι αγιω," and 3:5, "εαν μη τις γεννηθη εξ υδατος και πνευματος").

Chapter 7: The Power of Testimony

1. Louise Story, "Anywhere the Eye Can See, It's Likely to See an Ad," *New York Times*, January 15, 2007, http://www.nytimes.com/.

2. When the woman invites the men of Sychar to meet Jesus (4:28–29), she says that he "told me all the things I have done." John does not offer a transcript of this conversation, but a rendering. I believe his implication is that Jesus walked the woman through her past. I only intend what follows to dramatize what she could have faced and how Jesus might have treated such a history.

3. The manuscripts Sinaiticus (fourth century) and P66 (about 200 A.D.) both originally read, "I know that Messiah is coming." They were both corrected to read "we know." The correction indicates the magnitude of what the woman has said to Jesus. She no longer speaks about her community, but about her own beliefs. The ancient copyists assume this must be a mistake. She cannot possibly differentiate herself to such a degree. But the current consensus is that the original reading is correct. The woman now stands alone.

4. I interpret this statement as a claim of the divine name (cf. 8:58; 18:5–6). The emphatic nature of the Greek is clear: Εγω ειμι.

5. Most leaders in the various movements do not ascend to prominence with oversimplifications like these. I would be unfair if I charged most of them with consciously creating these subcultures. But the distinctives of the subcultures are really there. Assuming as I do that leaders have done what they felt was needed in good conscience, I am saying that new points of emphasis in all groups are absolutely necessary for the advance of the gospel.

Chapter 8: Be a Heretic

1. John Tierney, "An Early Environmentalist, Embracing New 'Heresies,'" *New York Times*, February 27, 2007, http://www.nytimes.com/.

2. The entire episode of John 6 should be read as a development of John's statement in 2:23–25. The masses believe because of a miracle (6:5–14), but Jesus knows their perverse motives (6:26–27).

3. The apologetics enthusiast in me notes that I have not yet established that the Bible is God's Word, that, in other words, I have skipped logical steps. But evading cultural boxes is not a matter of presenting an unimpeachable chain of inferences. It is a matter of presenting the listener with a cultural contradiction, and letting him or her wrestle with it.

Chapter 9: Find Your Mode

1. John Humphrys, "The Return of God?" *The Daily Telegraph*, March 3, 2007, http://www.telegraph.co.uk/.

2. Gillian Reynolds, "On Radio: A Rottweiler Goes in Search of His Maker," *The Daily Telegraph*, November 14, 2006, http://www.telegraph.co.uk/.

3. John Humphrys, "What I Found Out About God," *The Daily Telegraph*, December 23, 2006, http://www.telegraph.co.uk/.

4. Ibid.

5. Ibid.

6. Ibid.

7. Reynolds, "On Radio."

8. "Humphrys in Search of God," BBC Home, http://www.bbc.co.uk/religion/programmes/misc/insearchofgod.shtml.

Chapter 10: Answer the Question

1. Patricia Leigh Brown, "Supporting Boys or Girls When the Line Isn't Clear," *New York Times*, December 2, 2006, http://www.nytimes.com/.

Chapter 11: Confront a Friend

1. Daniel Goleman, "Flame First, Think Later: New Clues to E-Mail Misbehavior," *New York Times*, February 20, 2007, http://www.nytimes.com/.

2. This narrative conveys my own speculations, taking elements from many biblical passages and attempting to portray how Samaritan-Jewish hostility might have looked when the disciples were buying food for Jesus in Sychar. While I hope the attempt is plausible, given what we know from the Bible, I do not pretend it is definitive.

Chapter 12: Imagine the Scene

1. *Mother Jones*, September/October 2008, http://www.motherjones.com/.

2. Josh Harkinson, "Will Gay Marriage Help McCain?" *Mother Jones*, September/October 2008, http://www.motherjones.com/.

ABOUT THE AUTHOR

Matthew Raley is senior pastor of the Orland Evangelical Free Church in northern California, where he lives with his wife and two young children. For fun, he enjoys playing chamber music with friends, giving occasional solo recitals, and playing first violin in the North State Symphony. He is the author of *Fallen: A Novel* and writes a blog that can be found at http://tritonelife.com/.